faith

faith

Essays from Believers, Agnostics, and Atheists

edited by **Victoria Zackheim**

ATRIA PAPERBACK
New York London Toronto Sydney New Delhi

BEYOND WORDS
Hillsboro, Oregon

ATRIA PAPERBACK
A Division of Simon & Schuster, Inc.
1230 Avenue of the Americas
New York, NY 10020

BEYOND WORDS
20827 N.W. Cornell Road, Suite 500
Hillsboro, Oregon 97124-9808
503-531-8700 / 503-531-8773 fax
www.beyondword.com

Managing editor: Lindsay S. Brown
Editor: Emily Han
Copyeditor: Jennifer Weaver-Neist
Proofreader: Deborah Jayne
Design: Devon Smith
Composition: William H. Brunson Typography Services

First Atria Paperback/Beyond Words trade paperback edition February 2015

For more information about special discounts for bulk purchases, please contact Simon & Schuster Special Sales at 1-866-506-1949 or business@simonandschuster.com.

The Simon & Schuster Speakers Bureau can bring authors to your live event. For more information or to book an event, contact the Simon & Schuster Speakers Bureau at 1-866-248-3049 or visit our website at www.simonspeakers.com.

Manufactured in the United States of America

10 9 8 7 6 5 4 3 2 1

Library of Congress Cataloging-in-Publication Data

Faith : essays from believers, agnostics, and atheists / edited by Victoria Zackheim.
    pages cm
  1. Faith. I. Zackheim, Victoria, editor.
BL626.3.F35   2015
202'.2—dc23

                       2014031718

ISBN 978-1-58270-502-6
ISBN 978-1-4767-7253-0 (eBook)

The corporate mission of Beyond Words Publishing, Inc.: *Inspire to Integrity*

To Anne Perry,
for lighting my way on this journey

contents

Introduction

Have you ever been faced with an event so traumatic—the death of a loved one, the deception by someone you trusted, the suffering from a public humiliation—that you wondered if you would survive? Or if you wanted to? And then time passed, the pain eased, and life went on? Looking back, what was it that gave you the courage to move forward; to place one foot in front of the other; to choose action over stagnation, hope over cynicism? Was it your family? Your need to win out over adversity? Perhaps it was pride that drove you forward or the unwillingness to be viewed as a victim, prey to someone's cruelty. Or could it be that you came through this difficult time because you believed you could, because you had faith in yourself? Or in a force—an entity—more powerful than you?

It wasn't so long ago that I would not have asked these questions. In fact, any discussion of religion, spirituality, faith—and dare I say it: God—ran counter to everything I was taught by a mother who loathed religious doctrine. I cannot say for certain what shifted in me, what force or curiosity or awareness planted its seed in my heart and began to grow, but its presence was powerful enough to cause me to take notice. It also made me wonder if others shared my confusion, my struggle to understand.

As I contemplated this shift, thoughts of faith and what I believed increased. What role was faith playing in my life? Or did it play a role at all? And what, really, is faith? Is it religion? A belief in the goodness of humankind, in ourselves, our societies? I decided to contact a few writer friends and ask if they would be interested in writing about their faith. One writer, a friend of more than a decade and someone who I'd assumed was an atheist, informed me that she would *love* (emphasis hers) to write about her spiritual beliefs, while another friend, who used the name of God in much of her writing, informed me that she was a devout atheist, asking if she could write about that. Friend number three, a novelist who I'm quite certain would give up her life before giving up her faith, came back with such unbridled enthusiasm and support that I dared not turn my back on the idea. (Words like *smite* and *eternal housecleaning* came to mind!)

And now here we are, twenty-four writers opening our hearts and our minds as we share what we believe, prepared to reveal— in voices both hushed and loudly passionate—our most personal thoughts about faith.

The author and philosopher Søren Kierkegaard wrote, "The function of prayer is not to influence God, but rather to change the nature of the one who prays."[1] Must we pray to express our faith? And must faith always be tied to God?

In the process of creating this collection, I began to wonder if we redefine faith as we redefine ourselves. Perhaps ten people give it a different name yet feel it similarly. Some of the contributing authors believe in religious faith, while others do not. A good number believe in the kind of faith that comes from hope, while others eschew faith in all its definitions.

The polarization of faith is explored in this book. At one end is Malachy McCourt and his rant against all forms of religious beliefs; at the other is Anne Perry, whose faith embraces and sustains her through every step of her life. Dianne Rinehart uses the advent of advanced robotic technology to explain her concept of faith, while Rabbi Frank Smith introduces a faith-based organization of Muslims and Jews working to bring peace and balance to the Middle East. Beverly Donofrio writes about how faith saved her as she lifted her voice in prayer for the rapist who had attacked her—and was about to do so again. When he realized she was praying for his soul, he fled.

So many find their faith after decades of searching, while others discover that those beliefs drummed into them as children have lost their meaning as well as their power. David Corbett writes about shedding his faith after suffering the loss of his wife; Aviva Layton admits that she never had it, as much as she might have desired it.

In these essays, it's fascinating to learn how the writers' beliefs—religious or otherwise—are shifting as they move through the stages of life. Who has faith now where none existed? Who once believed in some power greater than humanity and felt it slip away? In any case, what did *faith* mean to them? Was it belief in the goodness of people, in the power of a deity, or perhaps an indefinable sense of something existing at the edges of consciousness? The force of the universe or the belief that the sun will rise and set each day.

Whatever the impetus, whatever the exigency of your journey, I invite you to ask yourself the two questions posed to all of the contributing writers:

What do you feel?

What do you believe?

faith

I

·———·

The day after Christmas 1985, I received a phone call that would change my life in a way I could never have predicted. It was mid-morning and I was home alone, enjoying a day free of client demands and killer deadlines. Political clients were on holiday from Congress, and my Silicon Valley clients, who were experiencing out-of-control growth and the kind of unlimited budgets that made freelance marketing writers very happy, were off to Aspen or Paris.

I picked up the phone with trepidation, fearful that someone from Hewlett-Packard needed brochure copy before noon, or that the marketing manager at Apple had been struck by another brilliant idea and could I write the narration for a new video before midnight? Instead, I heard the voice of my friend Lee. Our daughters were also friends—coltish teenagers as beautiful and smart as they were mischievous. Party

3

girls, fashionistas, and heaven only knew what they would do when old enough to drive. My Alisa was fourteen, her Lizzie was fifteen, and we commiserated (and plotted) about how to keep them safe. But this call was not about sneaking out to a party or concerns about too much eyeliner. "Lizzie's sick," she told me. "We're not sure what, but we're in emergency ... could you come?" Of all my friends, Lee was the least melodramatic. When I heard that plea, I ran to my car and made the thirty-minute drive in less than twenty, jeopardizing my safety and that of every other driver on the freeway. By the time I arrived at the hospital, Lizzie was surrounded by her mother, stepfather, and several of her stepfather's children. She was pale. Beyond pale. IVs were in place and pumping her with antibiotics, saline—anything to get her blood pressure to rise. We stood around her, curtain closed against the broken limbs and lacerations passing by. We stroked her and talked to her for hours, urging her to respond, reminding her of the seventy years of life that lay ahead. The monitor sounded and a young man in nurse's scrubs suddenly appeared. He climbed onto the bed, straddled Lizzie, and worked with a passion I had never seen before—and have not seen since—to resurrect her heartbeat. After nearly a quarter hour, Lee touched his shoulder. "She's gone. You can stop." He continued, back bent into the frantic pressing and releasing of hands against chest, and then his shoulders sagged and he climbed off the bed. We were too stunned to speak. Lizzie was fifteen—children are not supposed to die. A bacteria had invaded this beautiful child; the flu-like symptoms she had suffered on Christmas Day killed her one day later.

This death, following too closely the suicide of a friend's teenage son, left me angry and confused. I struggled to make sense of it—to go deep into my heart, my soul, to find some explanation, *anything*. But there was nothing there: no hope, no faith. Nothing. That place where hope once resided, where faith once teased and occasionally emerged, had turned into a dark space. I was empty, a conch with an echo where life had once lived.

I couldn't make sense of these tragedies; how could I explain them to my children?

I spoke at the funeral and recited a poem I had written for the occasion. As I stood before this child's family and friends—my lips moving, the words spilling out—I was aware of feeling nothing: my heart was numb.

Many years later, I read a poem by Frederic William Henry Myers and thought how painful it can be to desperately want to believe—to have faith in God, in any power—and to live with the fear that life could come and go without understanding what we believe.

A Last Appeal
Oh SOMEWHERE, somewhere God unknown,
Exist and be!
I am dying; I am all alone;
I must have thee!
God! God! my sense, my soul, my all,
Dies in the cry:
Saw'st thou the faint star flame and fall?
Ah! it was I.[1]

The writers in this book have accepted the challenge of exploring their thoughts, feelings, and beliefs, and for many, they've searched with more intensity and honesty than ever before. Some have seen "the faint star flame and fall"; others have not. And a few are still hoping.

A Secular Mystic

Tamim Ansary

When I was a kid growing up in Afghanistan as part of a family whose status in society derived largely from its religious credentials, *God* was a word I heard routinely. People didn't say, "Tomorrow, I'll do such and such." They said, *"If God wills it,* I'll do such and such." But no one ever specified who or what they meant by *God.* In devoutly Muslim Afghanistan, it was deemed unnecessary.

One day, however, when I was about five, I was playing with our neighbor's son, Suleiman, and he warned me not to do some naughty thing because God would grab me by the forelock, pull me up through the sky, and punish me. Evidently, the sky was a solid blue screen behind which God was always sitting, always watching, rather like those postal inspectors who watch mail sorters through one-way glass to make sure they're not opening people's letters.

I looked up and thought, *Okay, maybe the blue-screen idea is plausible*, but this other concept? Some powerful being sitting up there watching us? A being with arms that could reach, fingers that could grab, and a fanny that could sit? That, I had trouble buying.

I asked my American-born mother if it were true, and she gave me a circuitous answer about different people believing different things, and what I got from her hedging was no, it wasn't true. Suleiman's "God" was a myth. Only later did I have the vocabulary to understand that my mother was an atheist.

I did not grow up to be an atheist, but I didn't grow up to be a believer either, so what does that leave? Am I an agnostic? I think not. An agnostic is someone whose uncertainty concerns the existence of God. If I had to put a label on my faith, I would say I'm a secular mystic. Secular folks have no opinion about God's existence; they're busy with other matters. But a secular mystic would say, "The question is not 'Does God exist?' It's, rather, 'What do we mean by God?'"

Suleiman's picture felt implausible to me precisely because it was a picture—so specific, so physical. Suleiman seemed to envision God as one more creature in the universe, differing from lions, bears, and people only in being bigger, stronger, and more magically gifted—a superhero who might come to one's aid if only one obeyed and worshipped Him.

Even at five, this picture struck me as primitive, and today, when people talk about God, it's often this picture I get from their language. Quarterback Tim Tebow claiming that God helped him win football games made me picture God as part of the Denver team, like the coach, only higher. Yet when a columnist, jeering at Tebow's self-important version of humility, wondered why God would help Tim Tebow instead of ending world hunger, I got the same picture again. Because why would it be *instead of*? Doesn't God inherently imply omnipotence, omniscience, and ubiquity? Surely a power that cannot be here if it's there, and cannot be working on this problem if it's working on that problem, is not God but merely *a god*.

Let me go back to my neighbor Suleiman's picture of a powerful, vigilant supercreature. After soliciting my mother's view about this matter, I consulted my father, and he just smiled. A Muslim, he said, could not think of God as having arms or fingers, or grabbing a forelock, or sitting in some spot; these ideas were heretical. He told me about an ancestor of ours, Sheikh Sa'duddin, a Sufi mystic who wrote poetry under the pen name Turmoil of Love. "The Sheikh saw God everywhere," my father expounded. "He believed everything is God."

"Everything?" I gulped.

"Everything. He saw God in the trees, the clouds, the dirt—everywhere he looked, he said, 'This is God.'"

An intellectual sophisticate might say, if everything is God, is *anything* God? As a kid, however, I didn't parse the concept. It puzzled me but strangely thrilled me too. In the Koran, there's a line attributed to God that says, "I am closer to you than your own jugular." That's the feeling I got from my ancestor's maxim: closer than my own jugular.

I'll admit I didn't give it much thought after that, though, because what difference did it make to my daily life? None. If I was playing soccer, it didn't matter that the soccer ball was God; I had to keep the dribble going.

The sheikh's concept must have germinated in me, however. Years later, when I was going to school in America, my roommate, a voracious reader, tried to tell me about some philosopher he'd been devouring—Spinoza perhaps. He had trouble communicating the guy's ideas, however. "It's all One!" he finally spluttered. "Don't you see, Ansary? It's all One."

It's all One. The phrase resonated for me. It stirred up memories of my ancestor's Everything-is-God, but this slightly different semantic take directed my attention to the issue of interconnected-ness. *All is One* implied that every individual thing was part of the same larger something.

As it happened, around that time, I'd been mulling an intriguing scientific fact: my body was made up of cells, science said, but each of those cells was *a living unit in its own right.* Somehow, all those separate units added up to another single whole—me! What's more, according to science, the cells comprising *me* were constantly dying and being replaced by new cells. In fact, my material self saw a complete turnover approximately every seven years; not one cell in my body had existed seven years earlier, yet I felt like some single person with a continuous existence, moving through the universe, trailing my history. Who was this *I*? If, as the scientists claimed, not one material iota of my self had continuity throughout my life, what was the singularity I experienced as me?

Believers might label that enduring entity *the soul*. For me, *soul* carried too much baggage. The word *relationship* sufficed: what endured was the pattern of relationships. Just as a river forms stand-ing whorls and waves, even though not one single drop of water is the same from moment to moment, so my self was not some actual material thing but the standing pattern formed by the relationship among a multitude of cells washing through the reality of each moment like water in a river.

But if the pattern is what endures, where in the material realm is it located? Let me put it this way: If you put a dot on a page, you've got a dot on the page—a material entity. But if you put fifty dots on a page in a certain relationship to one another, you may have a circle (or the silhouette of a ship or a profile of Abraham Lincoln). In short, some new thing exists by virtue of all those dots, yet on the page there is still nothing but dots. Where, then, is the circle?

Scientific materialists would say the circle doesn't actually exist, it's *only* in one's mind, but that just begs the question. After all, the mental image of a circle dissolves upon analysis into neurons firing in a certain order, which are no different than those dots on the page. Neurons are the only material facts, and yet the circle exists. The circle is what those neurons add up to; the circle is what they *mean*.

The many adding up to one is, for me, the central mystery. Any single whole consists of meaning, not material. In this sense, the whole universe consists of meaning, for those dots on the page don't have material existence either. They, too, consist of smaller parts adding up to single wholes. It takes paper and graphite together to constitute a dot, but graphite and paper both dissolve upon scrutiny into molecules and atoms, quarks, and super strings. I exist only by virtue of my cells adding up to One, but my cells exist only by virtue of *their* parts adding up to One. It's meaning, meaning, meaning all the way down.

One day, these stray thoughts turned into an experience for me. It was brief but palpable. It was also indescribable, but I'll give it a go. I was walking along with a group of friends down a road lined with trees, beyond which were some low hills. I was noticing how my relationship to everything was changing as I moved. Then it struck me that, from my line of sight, the relationship of everything to everything was changing. At that moment, a vertiginous sense of plenitude overwhelmed me—a sense of how densely full of relationship the universe was. It contained no emptiness: everything was related to everything, and it all added up to One. And I was part of it.

After the catharsis faded, the idea remained, and I could not help but notice how perfectly it dovetailed with the proposition at the heart of Prophet Muhammad's revelation—his passionate insistence on the oneness of God. Most Muslims read that to mean that there is one God, and then—in addition—there is everything else. I reject that reading. To me, Islam is saying there is *no* separation between the many and the One; it all adds up. God is the singularity. Unity is the absolute and final truth.

Do I know this for sure? Of course not. This is not a knowable sort of proposition; it's a belief. It is my faith, if you will. My reading of the revelation of Islam differs from that of most Muslims, but it's right in line with the way the Sufi mystics have always read it. People like my ancestor became Sufis because, at some point, they had a jolting intimation of a unified totality that included them.

What good is this concept of God, some might ask? After all, religion has its functions. If nothing else, it is supposed to make people virtuous. How does the secular mystic's vision of God help illuminate the distinction between right and wrong? Help keep people from doing evil?

It doesn't. That's the secular part of a secular mystic. For me, ethical and moral questions belong strictly to the realm of human interaction. It's meaningless to say that a storm is evil or that a volcano shouldn't erupt. The issue of right and wrong is part of the never-ending negotiation among human beings, a conversation that can never end.

As a secular mystic, I base my quest for moral and ethical truth on loyalty to my fellow human beings, and I look to reason as my guide. I trace values back to deep principles, my conviction being that at the deepest level these principles are both rational and innate (to our species). Humans, as I see it, have two aspects: each of us is a biological organism but also a social entity, and we have imperatives related to both aspects of our nature. As biological creatures, we need to eat, procreate, stave off predators—do what's necessary to secure our survival, health, and growth. But as social entities, we also have obligations, duties, and responsibilities to others. Neither set of imperatives cancels out the other; we must hark to both.

In any given situation, the imperatives may conflict. There is nothing wrong with eating when you're hungry, but there may be something wrong with eating if someone you are with is starving. That's where a biological choice becomes a moral choice.

To my mind, discriminating between right and wrong is the distinctly human mechanism by which we negotiate between our two sets of imperatives. If we didn't have this mechanism, we would have gone extinct long ago. And the deepest underlying principle is simply this: the values we live by must enable us to live in harmony with our fellow humans, acting together as needed, while allowing each of us to fulfill our highest powers and potential. Ideally, we're looking to live by the principles of the highest possible community—the universal community, the closest we can come to the One. But none of us can really achieve this. We all live in some particular community, historically defined and limited. Most of us, therefore, find ourselves obliged, at times, to sacrifice ultimate ideals for ones that allow us to be moral people in a more limited here and now.

But our membership in the universal community (which includes all of humanity, all of life, all of nature) has to be the North Star for our values, the unreachable reference point by which we steer. When we adapt values to fit changing times and changing circumstances, it's not ultimate principles we're adjusting but the working values we use to keep our daily conduct in tune with these deepest principles.

Traditional believers often argue that if right and wrong don't trace back to an absolute authority outside the human sphere—to scripture, they mean—everyone is left free to do whatever they want, which is no moral system at all. But a secular basis for values, rationally pursued, can never ever end up as *everybody does whatever they want*, because that could never work as the guiding principle of *any* community, much less the universal one.

I think about Stephanie Strand, a member of a writing group I run. When Stephanie was about forty, she felt a vague pain in her abdomen but was too busy to see a doctor. When she finally found the time, it was too late: she had advanced uterine cancer. She did everything she could to stay alive—surgery, radiation, chemo—but nothing worked. Finally, she checked out of the hospital and went home to die.

She had a hospital bed in her room, and she got hooked up to nutrition tubes and medication tubes, but she needed someone to be with her around the clock and had no family except a young son, who had just joined the army and couldn't come home. So our writing group rallied. Working in shifts, we made sure at least one of us was with her day and night for the last few months of her life, keeping her company and attending to her needs.

It sounds lugubrious, but it wasn't. It was luminous, actually. Stephanie was good company to the end, and being with her put us in closer contact with one another. In her last month, Stephanie wanted to throw a good-bye party, and with the help of a friend who was a chef, she did. There we were, Stephanie in bed, hooked up to her feeding tubes, and all of us milling about, chatting, eating, drinking . . . the music played . . . the food was great—it was quite a good party, believe it or not. Afterward, Stephanie began hallucinating and a few weeks later she died.

Stephanie died young, it's true. But who's to say she died before her time? Most of her ambitions remained unfulfilled, nothing she wrote ever got published, and yet her death was a good one. She left the world surrounded by friends, and she managed to make none of us feel awkward or uncomfortable about the fact that she would soon be dead and we'd go on living. Also, she left us with the memory of what she had called forth in us.

I never heard any God-talk in Stephanie's house. I never heard anything about an afterlife. I don't know what she believed in that regard. We were not a church; we were a writing group—a secular group. But we took care of her because we're all human after all, and in the end I think that's what it's about: we're human beings—let's take care of one another. When I say I'm a secular mystic, that's what I mean by *secular*.

As for what I mean by *mystic*, let me try to get at this ungettable thing with one more story. Many years ago, my family and I went camping on Mount Lassen, California. My daughters were four and ten years old at the time. It was July, but winter had lasted unusually long that year, so parts of Lassen Park were closed by snow. We camped just below the snow line, on the border between summer and winter. Twenty minutes uphill from our campsite, we could ski and sled and snowboard. Twenty minutes downhill, we could swim in a warm lake drowsy with dragonflies, lily pads, and honeybees.

Next to our campground was a large pond encircled by a path, and one afternoon we decided to take a walk before dinner. Along the way, we stopped at a small cove to enjoy the view. When we were ready to move on, my four-year-old, Elina, resisted. Stoutly. She wanted to play some more right there.

I felt some impatience. I had entered upon this walk with a sense of purpose, a goal (to get back to where we started). But oh well. I told Debby and Jessamyn to keep going; I'd stay with Elina, and we'd catch up.

Elina went on squishing mud under her toes, and I sat peacefully by the water, and gradually, my impatience subsided. I relaxed about my goal. I allowed myself to just appreciate. I was grateful to Elina for making me linger. But then, at last, I had seen everything there was to see here and had done all the appreciating a man can do in one spot. Time to go.

Unbelievably, Elina was not ready. She pleaded with me to linger longer. I sighed and said, "Okay, a *little* longer." She went back to the mud and I went back to the view. I thought I had exhausted what there was to see, but it turned out there was so much more—subtleties I had not noticed before: the way ripples of light caught the tips of the waves to form a single shimmering pattern . . . the composition formed by snow-capped Lassen looming above the trees . . . and the smell of the air, a moisture in which snow and pollen were mingled . . . Wow, I would never have experienced all this had I hurried on. But okay, now we were done. Now we really had used up this spot. Night would be falling soon. We had to get dinner started. I said, "Come on, Elina. Let's go."

"Nooooo!" she howled. "Not yet, Daddy!" This time, her resistance was downright exasperating, and I was going to put my foot down, and yet . . . for some reason . . . I succumbed to her pleading once again. Just a few more minutes, I thought. But this time, when I sat back down, it was as if I had fallen through some screen and suddenly there were layers upon layers here—such depth, so much going on. In the air between Lassen and me hovered a shape-shifting cloud of gnats. Down at the water's edge, little water bugs with paddle-like legs were skimming the surface, busy with their tiny lives. From the branch of a bush hanging over them, a spider was constructing its web. A fish jumped in the water. The light on Lassen had changed because the sun was moving. A breeze across the waves ruffled those ripples of light. The color of the water had changed and was still changing because time was passing, night was falling, and now the gnats were dispersing . . .

How could I imagine I had exhausted this place—or *any* place? Every place was inexhaustible. And that's when something popped. Until that moment, I had been living in a stream of the events that constituted my life. Before I was here, I had been at the campsite, setting up our tent. After I left this place, I would be back at our site, building a campfire. Things had happened yesterday and the day before, and on back to the beginning, and things would happen tomorrow and the next day, and on until my death. Being here was one moment in a string of moments, and the string through all these beads was me.

But this spot had an ongoing life of its own. And just as this spot was an event in my life, I was an event in *its* life. This spot was here before I arrived and would be here after I departed. Things had happened here earlier and things would happen here in the future. And what was true of this spot was true of every spot: the entire, everlasting everything was going on right now and would go on going on. At some point in the future, I would stop existing—but not the universe. And to the extent that I was part of it all, I would not be gone either.

That thought gives me a comfort I have never gotten and, frankly, could never get from the prospect of an afterlife in which *I* will go on living. I do not want to go on living as my individuated self forever, even if it's in heaven. It pleases me to think that I will eventually be shuffled back into the deck and that new hands will be dealt. The deck is forever, and that's good enough for me.

What Do I Believe?

Anne Perry

What do I believe? It has been a long journey of discovery. There have been hesitations and errors along the way, and no doubt will be more, because I am still learning, both about myself and about life.

I have two voices within me. In my head there is that of my father. He was an astronomer and theoretical physicist. I remember him teaching me, when I was about three, that the sun was a star like any other and about nine minutes away at the speed of light. At the same time, he also taught me that Nazis and Germans were not necessarily the same thing. That was the more important of the two, especially since we were in London and it was the darkest days of World War II. The message was clear: don't label and don't judge.

He believed in the immeasurable beauty of creation and the love of knowledge, but not in a God. He looked at what man had done and continues to do in the name of religion, and he found it abhorrent. To him, kindness was the great virtue.

The other voice is in my heart, and it is that of my maternal grandfather, whom I knew only through the memories of my grandmother. He was a chaplain in the trenches during World War I (and the hero of my mystery series set in that time). My grandmother told me the stories of the New Testament in her own search for the same strength he had possessed. My favorite story was about Jesus taking time from his teaching to go and visit the sick daughter of Jairus, even though he had been told it was too late; the girl was already dead. He answered that she was only sleeping, saying to her, "Maiden, arise," and she awoke. Jesus even cared about sick little girls.

I was just such a sick little girl. On one occasion the doctor told my mother he would come back in the morning and sign the certificate of my death. But she would never give up. He returned to find my fever broken and me *arisen*. That story sank deeply into me, because I needed to believe that God cares for even the least significant of us.

As I grew up, I learned much of regular Christian teaching at school, and philosophy and morality at home. Perhaps most of us do. It was a time when courage, loyalty, honor, and kindness were the giants of virtue.

So what do I believe? It must make intellectual sense, even if my understanding is still incomplete. But more than that, it must make moral sense. How can I worship a God who is unfair? I cannot accept that anyone can be guilty without knowledge of both good and bad—or more likely, better and worse—and they must have the ability to choose. Blame without responsibility is inherently unjust.

Would God have created us, then told us not to seek knowledge of the difference between good and evil, and expected us to obey forever? Could anyone be so blind to human nature? And that doesn't even address the question of why he would wish us to remain innocent when it is essentially the same as ignorant, without growth or experience. That is the same as not being born at all. It makes the whole of existence purposeless. I can't accept that—I won't.

Surely it makes more sense that God knew perfectly well that sooner or later we would desire knowledge so passionately that we would take it, regardless of the consequences. But with knowledge comes accountability and the beginning of growth. And since we must abide both the good and the bad of that, it has to be our own choice. To me that makes sense and is the beginning of something beautiful, a mutual trust. A picture is emerging.

Then we come to the one question that really cannot be avoided. The big one, if you like. If there is a God, why is there such tragedy and chaos in the world? If he is all-powerful, he could prevent it. Does he not love us? Or is he simply not aware, not watching anymore?

Is it blasphemous to think that perhaps he is *not* all-powerful? Are there laws in the universe—moral laws that cannot be broken (just as the laws of physics cannot) without the universe flying apart and dissolving into the primal soup? No matter how much you love another person, you cannot grow for them either physically or spiritually. You cannot take their pain or prevent their failure. Ask any parent. You watch your children's stumbling steps, see them fall. But if you carry them all the time, they will never walk, let alone run or skip or dance.

Most of us struggle to explain the horrors we see or read about. Why are they allowed to happen? *Does hell have to be so very deep?* I wrote that question in a story once, and the response was immediate on my pen. *No, it doesn't, but if hell is less deep, then heaven is also less high. Is that what you want?* There was no hesitation in the answer, *No, it isn't.* That is the nearest I came to an explanation.

I believe passionately that the same power that protects me from hell, in doing so, denies me heaven. There can be no glory in the light without knowledge of the darkness.

I have considered the possibility that, in a way, all beauty of sense or hunger in the heart is not so much a difference in where we are but in our ability to perceive it. I think it was George Bernard Shaw who said that heaven is like a symphony concert hall: you can let anyone in, but you cannot make them hear the music. Learning to hear the music—all of it, every note—may be the exquisite refining of the spirit that takes much time, much experience, and much courage.

We need the passion of hope, the hunger for beauty that even a glimpse of it will bring. Heart and intellect should walk together.

Do I believe in the Christ of the New Testament because I want to so much? Am I afraid of a universe in which there is nothing beyond what I can see and someone can prove? Yes, I am afraid of it, but has that anything to do with truth or only with my perception of it? That cool voice of logic again.

Maybe I also believe it because I need to—the alternative is despair. I have certainly considered that possibility, especially at three in the morning when I feel small and miserable and desperately alone. Haven't we all?

I want companions in faith. Who wishes to walk alone? And yet I loathe hierarchy. There must be order in any organization or it falls apart and accomplishes nothing. But rank of importance suggests to me an essential inequality of existence, an unfairness.

That brings me face to face with my black dog of a word: *obedience*. I have no respect for disobedience nor for an instant do I advocate it. As children, we must begin by obeying. We are not safe to do anything else. But I want to move as fast as possible to the concept of learning, discovering, eventually doing the right thing because I understand it, I can see the beauty of it, and it is who I wish

to be! To do something because I am told to and will be rewarded
for it—or punished if I don't, or even to please God—is not a worthy purpose. It may have to be part of the process, but my goal is to
become the person who does the brave, honest, or kind thing because
it is my nature. It is not what I do; rather, it is who I am.

I want to be brave, not just look like it; be honest because I have
no wish to lie, above all to myself. I want to help others because I
see my own pain in theirs, and I want to ease it—for them, not for
me. It may be a long journey!

Recently I have given more consideration as to why the word
obedience scrapes me like a knife on glass. Am I really so obstruc-
tive? I have come to think it may hark back to a very impressionable
part of my childhood when the Nuremburg trials were being held
and Nazi war criminals tried to excuse themselves with the argument
that they were "obeying orders" and therefore not responsible for the
atrocities of the Holocaust. The judges at Nuremburg found differ-
ently—orders are not an excuse for anything. We have the dignity
and responsibility of being human, and all that that means. We are
responsible for our own decisions, our own acts. They may be mitigated but not ignored.

Then we come to forgiveness. I have to believe it is available
for everyone, without exception, but that does not mean there is no
price. I have read Dante's *Inferno* several times, and I find it one of
the greatest philosophical works of mankind because it shows so
vividly that we are not punished for our sins but by them. When we
do something ugly, cruel, or dishonest, we may hurt others, but it is
ourselves we diminish. We have become less than we were. In order
to heal we must change, become more again. Perhaps redemption
lies in understanding that, and being given the chance and the help
to do it.

It is so easy to philosophize. It sounds good. Forgive, as you
would be forgiven! I have a little exercise to help myself with that.

I imagine a dark, windy plain and a ring of people seated around a fire, so close together that the person outside cannot find any place to come in and belong again. No one will allow it. I can't bear it for him, whoever he is or whatever he has done. I see myself in him, and my rage goes. I can shut him out for a little while, but it can't last.

Do I believe that if we cannot forgive, then we cannot be forgiven? Yes, I do. Without compassion and the understanding to forgive, we have stunted ourselves irreparably; in fact, we have denied both life and hope. Perhaps that is what it all comes down to: love.

That brings me to another of my difficulties, the crucifixion of Christ. I have heard it said over and over that he died for each of us. But then the reasoning voice of my father reminds me that we all die, and uncountable numbers sacrificed their lives for others, willingly and knowingly, and many of their deaths were appalling. So what was different or more meaningful about Christ's death? Possibly nothing in the death itself. It was what happened in the Garden of Gethsemane before that is unique to him and changed eternity. Christ had a vision, taken outside time, in which he saw and experienced every guilt, grief, loneliness, and loss in the lives of all mankind, and yet, did not turn away but walked with us through each one.

I don't want to relive my own past griefs, illnesses, or guilts, let alone stand by helplessly and watch others'. There are pictures I deliberately do not look at, individual agony and humiliation, mass atrocity I refuse to see. I find watching one animal tortured almost more than I can stand.

In Gethsemane, Christ asked three of his disciples to watch with him, and for whatever reason, they could not. They fell asleep. If my watching with anyone through such pain would lessen it, would I love them enough to do it?

The greatest commandments of Christianity are *Love God* and *Love thy neighbor as thyself*. Perhaps the latter could also be said as *Watch with me*. There are griefs everyone faces at one time or another when a hand holding ours in the darkness is all that gets us through, and the promise *I will not leave you*.

We have our three-o'clock-in-the-morning moments when it is as if we are alone in the universe. The tides are drowning us. That is when we know who or what it is we really believe. I have surprised myself with how instinctively I turn to God.

The death of my mother left me feeling as if there were no longer anyone to whom I was so intensely important, who would know my mistakes and weaknesses, and love me anyway. The fear of a painful and possible mutilating illness or the fear of failure and loss of all kinds haunts us at these times.

The story comes to my memory of the woman who had had an issue of the blood for years and no doctor could heal her. She followed Christ through the streets of Jerusalem and touched the hem of his garment, with the faith that doing so, even without his knowledge, would heal her. He felt strength leave him and turned to ask, "Who touched me?" His disciples answered that the streets were thronged with people; it was impossible to know.

The woman came forward and said that it had been she.

His response was simple, "Thy faith hath made thee whole."

That story always moves me. I wish I had faith like hers, and I believe that if I did, I would be truly whole of spirit and soul, whatever my body did.

The more I study the history of mankind and the philosophies we have hammered out of our confusion and seeking, the more insistently do I hear the voice of my grandfather and the faith that survives and keeps you sane, without panic or despair even in the darkest night. If you cannot see the star any longer, remember that you once did and keep going. Follow where you know it was. Remember what was beautiful, and never lose it inside you.

Back to the beginning: Do I believe these things because I want to? Even need to? Perhaps, but it has a power and a beauty that I have found to work. Is that not the true, utterly rational, and pragmatic test? Does it work for me? Does it give me purpose, explain the darkness and failures of life, make me see myself and others as valuable, tender, capable of great good? Does it make me strive to love more, to be wiser, braver, gentler because I see the endless beauty of it?

Yes, it does—not every hour but at least every day. Of course I slip now and then; I forget. But then I remember the beauty, and there is a reason to start again.

There is an exercise through which I put some of my main characters. I picture them standing at the end of the world. It is a wild, blasted heath surrounded by volcanic darkness and universal destruction. Before them is Satan; beside them, the Abyss. He says to the character, "Tell me what you believe. Not what you have been taught by your parents or your spiritual leaders, but what you yourself will live or die for. If you tell me the truth, then I have no power over you. If you lie, you are going over the edge into the Abyss, and you are not coming back. Not here, not in eternity. Now speak."

I believe that the plan in which all human beings are the children of God and infinitely loved by him is the most beautiful thing possible. We have the opportunity to take mortal life upon ourselves, to learn and grow in wisdom, courage, honor, and the ability to love. To become more like God over the ages of time into eternity. This ought to be true because it is perfect. I desperately want it to be true because it makes sense of all I know, and it includes everyone and everything.

What else?

All the rituals in creation are of no use at all if you cannot be kind. That is what I am certain of.

What is in the little silver needle case that hangs on my bedroom door, written on a slip of paper and in my heart?

Be still, and know that I am God.

Love and Insomnia

David Corbett

I did not lose my faith so much as shrug it off, like a coat I'd come to realize wasn't up to the weather. I needed something sturdier, more reliable, something crafted more honestly and simply.

I had my suspicions about God as early as adolescence, only to see them confirmed for good during the darkest hours of my life. Fortunately, I discovered other resources to rely upon.

Some background: I was a blue baby and only survived birth through the determined intervention of the medical team at Mount Carmel Hospital in Columbus, Ohio.

This was back in the days when a mismatch of Rh factors between mother and newborn often proved fatal. My mother had almost died in childbirth with Jim, the second of the four boys, and her doctors had warned her against having more children. But

27

she was Catholic, and so both contraception and abortion were off the table.

Beautiful, curly-haired John ensued, with no complications, creating a bit of false optimism, perhaps. Then came me: Rh-positive to my mother's Rh negative, the beginning of a compatibility standoff that would never truly abate. While I hovered near death, the doctors ordered a full-body transfusion and complete quarantine, and my mother wasn't permitted to nurse or even hold me. I remained behind in the hospital for six weeks, a crucial period for mother–child bonding (another telltale sign of life to come).

I remember none of this, of course, nor do I remember the pediatric nurse who, according to family lore, developed such a devotion to me that she ventured into a blizzard on a municipal bus to deliver a Christmas present six months later: a scratchy wool bear I would unimaginatively name Teddy.

My first recollection is of clutching that bear (by then already one-eyed, with tufts of coarse fur missing) as I rose from my bed at night, unable to sleep. I might even say my self-awareness, my consciousness, was born in insomnia, which afflicted me nightly.

Emerging from the bedroom I shared with my brother John, I would first look right toward my mother's room. The door, as always, would be locked, with a washcloth wedged in the doorjamb to perfect its silence.

And so I turned left, toward the next room down, where my father slept. Each night, despite the long day behind him and the next one ahead, he rousted himself from sleep, slipped on his glasses, lifted me up, and with his pillow-mussed hair, took me into the living room and sat with me in the family rocker, where I perched in his lap and curled into his chest, clutching my poor, monocular bear, and gratefully rocked to sleep.

Looking back, this dynamic, established so early, became the framework of my life, my mind, and my character. On the one hand, a deep sense of unease abided within me, mitigated only by the stoic, patient, largely silent but reliably loving, concern of my father. On the other hand, my mother's extravagant moods—she suffered from borderline personality disorder and self-medicated with alcohol— would continue to nurture my anxiety and emotional uncertainty. Her affections were devout but dramatic, unpredictable, freighted with need. In a family of scared men, she reigned all but absolutely. The role of lone apostate deferred to me.

Though I secretly longed to be closer to her, I never trusted her, often feared her, and, I'm ashamed to admit, at times even despised her. The saccharine, manipulative endearments she used to beguile my father and brothers seemed a kind of black enchantment, and I pledged myself to leaving home as soon as circumstances allowed.

Ironically, I wasted much of my early romantic efforts unwittingly searching for her duplicate. I could not recognize love except in seduction and turmoil. Through her, I suppose, I learned the humbling power of the unconscious and its eerily invisible control over my behavior. Fortunately, I would also learn—later and elsewhere—the power of insight and acceptance, and the genuine possibility of change.

But I'm getting ahead of myself.

My changing relationship with my brother John reinforced the curious dynamic with my mother. In the beginning, John and I were quite close. He was three years older but he looked after me, played with me, introduced me to the other kids in the neighborhood, and served as my protector. Then, about the time he entered Catholic school, he changed. He recognized he was different, and long before he knew the words *homosexual* or *gay*, he felt a special type of scrutiny. With no way to express the increasing sense of dread and shame and guilt he felt, he projected those feelings onto me.

Just as my mother routinely shamed, degraded, and criticized my father, so John began a reign of terror with me, finding fault with

absolutely everything I did. The other family members often joked
about how capably I handled this onslaught of criticism, not realizing how much it was misshaping me inside.

The message I learned was this: only perfection guarantees love.
And I knew I was hideously, sloppily, perfectly imperfect.

This message was echoed at Catholic school. We were made in
the image of God, we were told, and since God was perfect, anything
less than perfection was unacceptable. Even children—especially
children, to some minds—were rank with sin. And though God in
his mercy (the argument went) could forgive us and, after death,
embrace us, this always felt like a long shot. We were taught to hate
ourselves and "the weakness of our nature." We were the banished
children of Eve, mourning and weeping in our vale of tears.

Not surprisingly, my role as family heretic followed me to school.
I never quite fell for the company line in either domain, though I rel-
ished the Bible stories and proved adept in the rigors of catechism.
While several of the priests and nuns I met were truly decent—even
admirable—far too many were sanctimonious bullies, the best of
who admittedly possessed a kind of mercurial, benevolent-but-cruel
strength, something I'd later recognize as the hallmark of fascism.

Far more often than not, though, it seemed the more devout the
patter, the more spiteful and meager the spirit. If a life devoted to
God created such misshapen, punitive, unhappy souls, I thought,
who but a fool would bother?

To top all that off, the vast majority of the truly exceptional
priests and nuns I met ended up surrendering their vows or left the
church altogether.

But the beauty and majesty of faith—the intellectual rigor of
Augustine and Ambrose and Aquinas, the courage of the martyrs and
missionaries, the spirit that inspired Gregorian chant and liturgical
polyphony and the Masses of Bach and Mozart, not to mention the
Sistine Chapel and the great cathedrals of Europe—this I couldn't

shake off so handily. Who was I to question the ineffable something that drove so many to such excellence?

I walked that tightrope through my twenties and early thirties, when I began to pursue my artistic inclinations seriously and blundered through a series of stormy relationships and erotic misadventures, careening into my adult selfhood.

Meanwhile, my relationship with my brother John improved markedly. We reconciled after he came out, forging a warm though not entirely untroubled bond once he decided that a God who loved him couldn't possibly want him to be as miserable as he'd been as a boy, and so he accepted both his homosexuality and his faith.

Unfortunately, he was mistaken. Apparently his God did want him—and an entire generation of smart, generous, creative men like him—to be miserable, to waste away before our eyes, to die slow, agonizing deaths at the mercy of AIDS, a plague of biblical proportion, while the sanctimonious bullies all but cheered.

My other older brothers—more conservative than John or I—had by now turned away from Catholicism and embraced evangelical Protestantism. They spoke of surrender to God and wisdom through acceptance of his inscrutable will. But after having watched John wither and die so helplessly and horribly, the thought of accepting this as God's will seemed like a puffed-up, pious version of the same cowardly mumbo jumbo that had justified the family subservience to an extravagant drunk. I knew God wasn't my mother, but they had a similar approach to those they claimed to love: do what I want or I'll make your life wretched. Whatever such a God might be, he was without doubt unworthy of worship.

As it turned out, John's death forced me to look more deeply for some kind of understanding of my life.

From a therapist I'd grown to trust, I gained two of the most important insights of my life. First, after a debilitating series of episodes where I increasingly found everything and anything I wrote utterly worthless, I descended into an acidic despair in which I came to believe nothing I ever did (and certainly nothing I wrote) would ever bring me happiness.

Therapy pointed a way out of this pit of self-loathing. Curiously, it came in the form of an insight I might have dismissed at another time as hopelessly sentimental and trite. But at this juncture, it saved my life: the perfect is the enemy of the good. I came to forgive myself for the sin of being me. I learned to strive to be better without lashing myself with self-doubt and contempt. I broke the chain of perfectionism that bound me to both my family and my faith.

Second, I came to understand that, despite all the emotional gamesmanship I'd endured growing up, I'd known unconditional love as well, and it, too, had saved me. Its source was my father. Perhaps, my therapist suggested, I'd be happier if I began seeking a relationship with someone more like him than my mother.

It was through taking this advice to heart, and with John's recent death deepening my understanding of the fragility of this existence, that I met the first great love of my life: Cesidia Therese Tessicini. We met by accident and very shortly decided we were meant for each other, to the extent that human beings can claim such things.

Our marriage provided me the happiest, most rewarding years of my life. Like my father, Terri (as she was called) was gentle, caring, and utterly decent. She was also playfully silly and, true to her Italian heritage, stubborn to the core.

We were both the children of problematic mothers, so we mothered each other. I, who had never trusted my mother, learned that there are indeed people who are fundamentally honest, and such a person could love me. Terri, so fearful of betrayal and abandonment, learned that there are indeed people who are fundamentally loyal, and such a person could love her.

Simply put, the devotion Terri and I shared made God and perfection irrelevant. Everything I had wanted of my existence, our marriage provided. I'd found someone I loved without question, and watched as that affection and commitment transformed Terri from a shy, soft-spoken "wounded bird" (as a friend described her) to a strong, confident, successful "barracuda" (as one of her legal clients referred to her). In return, I was seen for who I was and I was loved honestly. I was cared for. For the first time in my life, I felt safe.

I wasn't, of course. Or rather, Terri wasn't. Around the time of her forty-sixth birthday, she began treatments for what was first believed to be a reaction to cortisone shots she'd received for a problematic shoulder. But abdominal pain contradicted that diagnosis, so she had a complete physical, during which a savvy nurse practitioner performed a sonogram. It revealed a complex mass in Terri's ovary.

Within a matter of weeks, she was diagnosed with Stage IV clear cell epithelial ovarian cancer. Four months later, she was dead.

The devastation I'd felt after John's death was nothing compared to what followed Terri's passing. In the magical thinking so common to grief, I began to wonder if I wasn't a jinx to those I loved and those who loved me. More to the point, I couldn't imagine life ahead as anything but an interminable wait. Death wins, I realized, and that seemed the only rock-solid wisdom to be had.

I wasn't so much bitter as lost. As days ground into months, I realized that the depression I was battling served no real purpose. I wasn't honoring Terri, and I was crippling myself.

As it turned out, two things Terri said before dying ended up pointing me in the right direction. The first was her insistence that I promise to take care of our three dogs. Terri had been the oldest sister in a family of four kids, and in a household where parenting was unpredictable, she became a mother to her two younger siblings. They even followed her when she left home as a teenager. And so she'd had her fill of motherhood but not of family, and the dogs became our brood.

I realize that seems hopelessly bourgeois, but I know for a fact that those dogs saved my life. Through them I learned the secret of

escaping depression: it ain't all about you. Having someone to care
for other than myself provided the crucial element in climbing out
of the despair in which I'd become mired.

The other gift from Terri was a letter she wrote that I was not
allowed to read until after she passed. In it she told me that she had
no words to express our love: "It just was." She wanted me to cry
her a river, then grab life by the tail and never let go. "I want you to
marry again, and she'll be the luckiest woman in the world."

Because of that letter, I realized that our love would only die if I
let it. If I remained strong enough and wise enough to keep allowing
the example of our marriage to change me for the better—if I carried that love forward into my seemingly empty life—the emptiness
would dissipate.

Some books came in handy as well. Yeats, Robinson Jeffers,
Anna Akhmatova, Donald Hall, Kim Addonizio, Dorianne Laux—
in their poems they all addressed death and loss in ways that spoke
to me profoundly and personally.

A good friend gave me *When Things Fall Apart* by the Buddhist
nun Pema Chödrön, and that book changed me utterly, obliging me
to reflect more deeply, honestly, and bravely on death and annihilation: impermanence. It also taught me how fiercely we grasp at our
worldly gratifications, only to lose them. Wisdom lies in letting go,
while caring no less.

I once and for all threw off the supposed solace of God. I recognized the sneaky deceit in believing there was a hand to reach for,
a hand to hold, rather than accepting the inherent ambiguity of this
existence. And yet that ambiguity doesn't mean life is a pointless,
cheerless, terrifying exercise in endurance. On the contrary, whatever meaning life possesses is mine to discover or create.

From all of this, with additional insight gained from my writing,
I devised a simple way to live. In a sense, I let my life imitate my art.

As my writing matured, the characters who inhabited my stories increasingly exhibited an underlying yearning to be more courageous, more honest, more loving. *If true of them*, I thought, *why not me*?

I also recognized that my characters came to life most vividly, not in self-reflection, but in their engagement with others. And that led me back to a humble truth I'd learned from a friend in my twenties: you don't know yourself by yourself.

Honesty and courage and love are intertwined, mutually dependent, and none is a solo effort. We learn the truth about ourselves and muster the will to go on through our engagement with the world, our relationships—our loves.

And so I devised a practice of trying each day to reflect on how I might become just a bit braver, more truthful, more caring. In trying to observe those three simple virtues and to use them as a guide in how I interact with others, I found a way to both embrace my life and accept my death.

Not that all problems are solved, of course. I still suffer from insomnia, sometimes waking in the early morning hours with a gnawing dread. Fear is biological and it favors the dark. It's a condition, like sleeplessness. And yes, the death of my brother and my wife left an indelible impression, one not even mindfulness can extinguish.

I'm still the extravagantly flawed and frightened person I've always been, though I'm perhaps a bit better at working the pedals of this machine of meat called me. Regardless, I've found that simply getting up and beginning my day dispels a great many shadows. Dread, like everything else, passes.

I've also found love again, and with someone as extravagantly named as Ms. Tessicini: Mette Hansen-Karademir. Once again—like my father—she's decent and caring, practical and honest. Once again—like Terri—she's stubborn and smart and playful. Why buck a favorable trend?

I know I will lose Mette, and she will lose me. I know chances are good that it won't be easy or pretty for either of us; I think about this every single day. And when the fear rises up, as it always does, I think of how I might be just a little bit braver, more honest, more caring. This is the practice I've devised, to replace the faith I found lacking. I live my imperfect, impermanent life. Or rather, I share it.

II

I was in high school and believed I controlled my life, knew where it was going, and how best to arrive there. I had telephoned a classmate, Margo, whose mother was coming home that day from the hospital. It was my friend's sister who answered and, sobbing, managed to convey that her mother, while preparing to check out, had suddenly died. I ran around the corner to tell a mutual friend, and there was Margo walking toward me, waving and smiling. As she neared, I pulled her into our friend's house and insisted she call home. This was fifty-five years ago, yet I clearly recall her face as she learned of her mother's death—see how it collapsed into disbelief and then grief. My father brought our car around and I sat in the back with Margo, holding her as she wept. It was in those ten minutes in the car that she became suddenly calm, explained that she would miss her mother terribly, deeply, but that she would bear that loss because her mother was now home with God, where she had always hoped to be.

Until that day, I was unfamiliar with such convictions and felt confused. Over the months that followed, I recognized how Margo's faith comforted and sustained her. But how was that possible? It ran against everything I had been taught by a mother who felt that anyone who believed in God—or in any power greater than humanity's—was stupid. Even as a little girl, I knew in some wise place that people's beliefs were their own, and therefore right for them, but I never challenged my mother. My wisdom also informed me that this was an argument I would never win.

Have you ever experienced a shake-up in your life so profound that you began to question your life—the direction it was taking you—and wondered how to regain control? I've certainly had my share of sleepless nights and of stumbling through days as endless as a hostile desert, and finally emerged from this miasma, stunned and confused, to try to redefine what life is about—what I am about. I find myself wishing my mother were here so we could continue that conversation. There are so many questions I'd like to ask, so many arguments I could now enter into with knowledge and wisdom to support my positions. Sadly, neither this meeting nor this debate will ever happen.

Choosing

Beverly Donofrio

I'm thirty-three and living with my seventeen-year-old son in a fifth-floor walkup in Alphabet City in New York City. The bathtub is in the kitchen, the toilet's in a closet, there's only one table in the whole place, and the floor slants so much that a marble on a roll could kill a cockroach.

Living in New York is my dream come true. I was a teen mother who'd finally gotten into college, graduated five years ago, then moved to the city to be a writer. I've been working menial, part-time jobs to preserve precious time at the typewriter, but I'm usually too tired, depressed, scared about money, and hung over to write much of anything.

Down below, on Avenue A, buses wheeze exhaust fumes, and through the windows the air drops so much grime onto the white

Formica table my son and I eat on and I write on, I can draw my name in it. Looking out the windows, I'm reminded of a favorite TV show when I was a kid, *Naked City*: "There are eight million stories in the naked city, and this is one of them." In the only episode I actually remember, a woman screams for help on the street, but no one in the buildings towering above lifts a finger to help her. Looking out my windows, I witness a knife fight between two men of radically unequal heights, until blood blooms round the knife in the short one's belly and he falls to his knees; I hear a woman scream, "Help!" and watch as a man pulls her along the sidewalk by her hair; boys run down Twelfth Street shooting guns, "Did you get him? Did you get him?" Unlike the people in *Naked City*, I seem to call the police every other Saturday night.

I do not call the police the time, one summer Sunday morning, I see a baby fall from her fourth-floor window, her yellow dress billowing like a parachute. My windows are open, but I hear no sound. People gather around her and reach their hands like she is a fire they dare not touch. Finally, a police car screeches to a halt; a cop jumps out, wraps the baby in his jacket; and the siren screams as they speed off.

That siren call to arms ricochets off the walls of my apartment the entire summer. I don't know if I am more angry because I live in a world where such tragedies can happen or because I have the bad luck to be looking out the window at exactly the right moment to witness the horror. I am furious at a God I haven't believed in since adolescence. I weep for the baby, her mother—for every sad, senseless event I carry in my litany of evidence of how cruel and unfair and scary life is. I decide (not for the first time) that even if God does exist, which of course he doesn't, I'll have nothing to do with his sadistic ass.

•————•

Seven years later, I'm forty years old, and so many dreams have come true. I'm a published author with money in the bank, a contract to write another book, and a motion picture in the works. I've just moved to an old whaling village, where I know no one. I live alone in a lovely Victorian with a view of the bay and think I should be happy, but I'm filled with longing—a homesickness for something I can't even name. I never get out of bed some mornings, and eventually become desperate enough—finally—to begin meditating. My new therapist suggests guided meditations in which I imagine God, an angel, spirit, saint, whatever appeals, loving me unconditionally. I dream up a lovely young Persian woman who flies me around on a carpet and bathes me in streams.

A few months later, it's spring, and I go yard sale-ing. At my first contents-of-house sale, I spot the Virgin Mary as Our Lady of Fatima, standing on a cloud that could be a rock, the sky gray and twinkled with stars. A rosary is draped over her praying hands and three kids kneel on a grassy hill, looking up at her adoringly. It's only a framed postcard, but you'd think it was the Mona Lisa by the speed at which I snap that Mary up. After that, I'm on the road by 7:45 every Saturday morning on a hunt. I collect so many paintings, statues, and rosaries, my house could be a shrine.

"What's up with all the Marys?" my friends want to know.

"They're cheap. Kitsch," I tell them. "Beautiful, though, don't you think?"

Secretly, I begin to wonder and then gradually admit only to myself: Mary in my house makes me feel (dare I even think it?) a little lighter, less frightened, more safe.

Evidence: I dance all the time.

• ———— •

I'll be fifty in the year 2000, and as the turn of the century approaches, a wave of fear builds around the country and maybe the world. People fear computers will crash, planes will fall from the sky, bank systems will go berserk, losing everyone's money—and, like the Good

Witch Glinda in *The Wizard of Oz*, the Virgin Mary comes to the rescue (sort of). Her image on a Washington State billboard ties up traffic for hours. Three-stories tall on the windows of a glass office building in Florida, no matter what solvent is used, she will not be washed off. People spot her on tree trunks, picture windows, taco shells. I develop a theory: people see Mary when they're frightened and need a mother. Or perhaps Mary comes when people are open to a mother's love. The last thing anyone needs is to feel judged, which is what the Judeo-Christian father—God—offers; they need to feel nurtured.

I do some research and find there are Virgin Mary apparition sites around the country, and then visit a few for an NPR documentary I write and narrate. My first stop is my parents' house in Connecticut, where my mother is hooked to oxygen on the sofa, pale and tired, every breath a trial. She could use another Virgin Mary miracle like the one she told me about when I was little. I've come with my producer so Mom can tell it on the radio.

When she was twelve, my mother went swimming in a lake with her cousins one weekend and began to drown. She'd just lost her mother, and an aunt with two children had taken her in. She missed her mother terribly and felt unfairly treated, like Cinderella. Sinking under the water for the third time, she saw the Blessed Virgin Mary glowing in the sky, her arms stretched out to her. The next thing she remembers, she awoke on the beach, saved.

Now, when I ask my mother to recount her Virgin Mary story, she says, "It wasn't Mary; it was my mother."

"Mom!" I'm shocked. "You told me it was Mary." I don't think I would have made that up.

She looks confused for a moment and then, as though a shade spins open, "You're right!" Color actually returns to her cheeks. "You probably think I'm nuts, but it was her. So peaceful. I can't describe. It was the Virgin Mary."

Her misremembrance seems to prove my theory: my mother had wanted a mother.

At the apparition sites there is usually a seer, someone to whom Mary appears, and who hears motherly messages, such as, "Be nice. Stop fighting. Love your brothers and sisters." People gather around the seer at an appointed hour, pray Hail Marys, and some witness miracles. They tell me stories of being at death's door, losing everything, hitting rock bottom, wanting to die. They "surrender," beg for help, and are given "tremendous graces."

"What do you mean by *graces*?" I ask each time.

"Peace," they say.

"I don't feel angry anymore."

"I healed from MS, cancer . . . hemorrhaging . . . migraines . . ."

"Pray the rosary," so many advise me. "It will change your life."

What if Mary is really around and involved, helping us?

I want this to be true, and at this point, to pray the rosary is not such a stretch. A few months before, I'd sold practically everything I owned to live with a friend of a friend in L.A. and bank on my first memoir's movie finally getting made. I'd prayed so many Hail Marys to keep myself calm on the drive across the country, if you'd laid them end to end, they'd reach China. But there's one big problem: like all my friends, I equate Christians with right-wing, abortion-clinic-bombing right-to-lifers who quote scripture to support homophobia and the death penalty. I'm afraid that if I turn into a believer, every friend I have will dump me like the dregs in yesterday's coffee cup. But for the sake of the documentary (or so I tell myself), I'll pray an entire rosary every day, with the hypothesis that if I act as though I believe, belief might follow. Also because I *like* saying Hail Marys.

I finish the documentary, but I'm not finished with Mary. I propose writing a book, for which I will go to Medjugorje, Bosnia, the grand kahuna of Virgin Mary apparition sites. On the pilgrimage I will fast on bread and water with forty-eight rabid Catholics and be silent for seven days, before leaving for a miraculous-sites-of-Italy tour. A week before I travel to Bosnia, my palms break out in a hideously scaly rash that itches like a thousand mosquito bites. I assume this is from sheer anxiety. Then, as soon as I board the plane to Medjugorje, the itching stops. Every inch of skin peels off my palms—to make way for a new identity, I'm convinced. In Medjugorje I have a full-blown conversion experience: I see the sun spin, silver medals turn gold, a tear disappear from a Mary statue, and I cry like a baby, more sorry than I can ever say for all the pain I've inflicted, the hate I've felt, the love I didn't give. I know I must forgive myself and everyone else. I feel like an infant in her mother's arms every time I enter a church. Mary has become an everywhere, all-enveloping, ever-present, wholly loving mother, the feminine face of a God who loves you not because you're good but because it's what She does. My experience is much like a priest told me several years later: "It's like hearing about your friend's friend, compared to meeting the friend. You don't understand God, you know God."

For me, through Mary, God is rain in the desert, a hand in the ocean, the hush after a hurricane. God would also become a dog dancing at my feet, the sound of a tree falling in the forest, gales, tsunamis, floods, an old lady bent in half, my own breath—everything that makes me know I'm alive.

•———•

To write the book I've proposed about the Virgin Mary, I go to Mexico, which makes perfect sense: In Mexico, Mary's above more altars than her son, Jesus Christ, and in San Miguel de Allende, the town I write my book in, "Ave Maria" is played at noon every day on the radio; Mary's statue is paraded around the streets in the backs of pickup trucks, hoisted on pallets, passed around for stays in people's homes. In Mexico you greet people and say good-bye with *Adiós*, which means "to God." "God is alive in Mexico," I tell everyone who'll listen. I write my book, and then I move there permanently and build a house.

I dance salsa, drink margaritas, run a lecture series, hike, do yoga, have Sunday-night HBO viewings at my friends'—cannot find enough days in the week to fit in all my new and old, always-interesting friends. Seven years pass, and as the white heat of my conversion experience fades like fabric in the sun, I still pray Hail Marys in English and in Spanish, attend vespers at a Benedictine monastery, meditate at Yogananda services, paint icons in silence with a friend, read the New Testament, books on Christian contemplative prayer, Buddhist practice and philosophy, and anything by Thich Nhat Hanh. I'm convinced that love possesses the highest vibration, and fear, the lowest. Aware that thoughts have power and wanting to affect the world in a positive way, I try—and fail—to discipline my mind toward gratitude and away from criticisms, fear, anger, envy, hate.

Then my grandson, Zachary, is born and I feel such a rush of love that my heart catches fire and lights up everything: *What's important? What am I doing with my life? What have I been missing? What can I do to infuse the rest of my time on this planet with even a bit of the radiance I felt at Zach's birth? What can I do to create or to find significance and meaning?* The answer seems to be to love more, love always, love everything. I decide to dedicate the rest of my life to love, which, for me, means to God. This will require a miracle and discipline. At least discipline is something I have control over: I will develop it by living the *Rule of Saint Benedict* at a monastery. With my sisters I'll pray the sun up and down; pray for the poor and the lonely and the lost; make work—indeed *every* act—a form of prayer; pay closer attention to every minute, event, and person, which will mean making God the focus of the rest of my days.

I have faith that this will happen. I have heard faith defined as "to set one's heart on."

This is precisely when a serial rapist slips into my bed. "Don't scream; I have a knife," he says, in such a tone you'd think he's bored, as though he's used it many times before—which he actually has. I will be his fifth known victim in eight months. People in town have mail ordered mace and made their own pepper spray; they've installed bars on windows, put their houses up for sale, fled because of this man.

I know from the experiences of his other victims, two of whom I'm friendly with, that if I fight, I'll get beat up; if I don't fight, I won't. So, I cross my arms on my chest, turn my face away, and the physical attack is over in two minutes. Afterward he wants to talk, as I'd heard he would, in a sick perversion of postcoital intimacy before he rouses himself for another round. Like a prisoner hearing his buddy being tortured in the next cell, I dread the rest of the evening. I decide to check out and pray. I begin a Hail Mary, then in seconds it occurs to me to pray out loud and maybe freak the rapist out.

"You're praying," he barks, pounding my shoulder with his fist. "Stop praying."

"I'm praying for *you*," I bark back, which is a lie I realize I should make the truth. And so I pray for him, which helps me remember to pray for myself. As I pray the Hail Mary out loud, inside I beg Mary, God, Jesus, the Holy Spirit, every dead relative, angel, and saint to get this man the hell out of my bed and out of my house. He backs out of the bed, pats my shoulder, says, "It's okay, I'm leaving," and lets himself out.

I write about it in the local paper, and the article is accompanied by the Hail Mary in English and Spanish. Notices appear in stores around town, "Our sister Beverly was raped. She prayed the 'Ave Maria' and so should we." People cut the prayer out, keep it by their beds, carry it in their bags, memorize it, pray it. Five days after the article appears and people begin praying, the rapist is caught.

Above my bed are a dozen icons I'd painted of Mary. Uncon-
sciously I'd believed that they, along with all my spiritual practices,
would keep me safe. After my rape, I cry tears that don't stop for
years. I wake up too many nights screaming, because I believe an
evil presence is hovering over my bed, even after I open my eyes.

•———————•

I go on retreat to five different monasteries and houses of prayer.
Then I settle into a Carmelite hermitage and retreat center in the
Sangre de Cristo Mountains of Colorado, where I eventually take
vows as a lay member.

I've had enough derailments in my life—and now have read
enough mystics whose books leap into my hands in the library—
to know that the most scary, disruptive, painful events can create
opportunities to change and grow. Great pain and great love are two
universal pathways to God.

I meditate three times a day, hike the mountain outside my window, practice hatha yoga, watch the sun rise and the sun set, study
mystics from many traditions. I see a bobcat take out a bunny, two
porcupines waddling down my dirt road, coyotes walking the ridge
outside my window, herds of deer staring at me, and in the chapel, I stare at the almost life-size ascension crucifix: Jesus on the
cross, in transit to bliss. I resist Jesus and his martyrdom, his role
as scapegoat, am infuriated at being made to feel guilty because he
"died for our sins." Who asked him to? I even deride the cannibalis-
tic injunction to eat his body and drink his blood in remembrance of
him until the act of receiving the communion host floods me with
such warmth and gratefulness, I either fight my tears or cry, almost
every time.

I come to so love and admire the saints and mystics I've been
spending my days and nights with, reading and contemplating—
Saint Teresa of Avila, Saint John of the Cross, Brother Lawrence,

Saint Therese of Lisieux, Thomas Merton, Bede Griffiths—that I
try following their examples and opening to Jesus. It helps that the
Jesus depicted in this chapel looks like his name could be Stanley.
His body straining off the cross, his face caught in the split second between agony and ecstasy; Christ seems so human, and it's
his humanity—that he is human *and* divine—that helps me. I don't
believe I'm called to worship Christ but to follow him: to be as he is,
to do as he does, to love my neighbor as myself, to forgive and forgive, to know that the kingdom of God in all its abundance is right
here, right now—if I only have eyes to see it.

This quote from Rumi says so much about my life—any life—
which I now think of as God:

If you hit a porcupine with a stick, it extends its
quills and gets bigger. The soul is a porcupine,
made strong by stick-beating.

And this is how I become grateful for the rape.

•———•

I leave the monastery to return to the world. I move back East, to
be near family and old friends—and to write a book about my rape
and the spiritual journey that healed me. The book is published;
I settle in Woodstock, New York; and I receive an email from a
friend in San Miguel de Allende. She tells me how a close friend
of hers, a Mexican woman, was kidnapped. The kidnappers grabbed
her at her front gate, blindfolded her, tied her up, and threw her into
the backseat of their black Suburban. They drove around all day
threatening her and demanding money from her husband, who had
consulted experts on abduction and been told to give the kidnappers
nothing. Meanwhile, the wife pleaded with her abductors, claimed

poverty, pleaded all day, and then remembered the story she'd heard about the woman who'd been raped and prayed Hail Marys. Now, she did the same—loudly. She never stopped. The men stopped threatening and became kind. They didn't touch her or handle her roughly. And they released her.

The woman was not religious but believed that all Mexicans at some level believe in the Virgin. The woman asked my friend to tell me she is sure her prayers saved her and to thank me. My friend adds in her email, "My intention is to share the brilliancy of her strategy, not because the Virgin saved her but that she was smart enough to pick the soft spot in [the violent men], as you did."

I have yet to meet the woman, but I know: in that time of fear and desperation, she didn't only pray the words out of a clever stratagem but begged with all her heart, hoping there is a God out there listening.

"Do not be afraid," is the most repeated phrase in the Bible; I remind myself of it almost every day. And to do this, all I have to do is see abundance everywhere—in you and me and everything. Even a rapist.

Ah. Yes.

Amy Ferris

*H*e *was a spiritual advisor/therapist of sorts. More like a healer/
shaman. I had known him for years. I told him that I felt empty,
lost . . . completely depleted. "I think I need to reconnect with a spiritual path," I said. "It finds you," he told me. "One day you'll be doing
something, standing somewhere, driving in the car . . . and you'll just
feel it, get it . . . know it. You'll know it. It'll wash over you."*

"Oh," I said, "you mean like an aha moment."

*"More like an ah-yes moment. Aha is a light bulb; ah-yes is the
whole wiring system. It's not a fall-to-my-knees moment; it's pure
clarity."*

•———•

It was sort of like an impulse buy.

51

There was a period when I was feeling this overwhelming need to fill a huge void in my life. I wasn't quite sure what the void was; I just knew that something—something—had to fill it.

And then I knew.

• ——— •

I remember that morning as if it were yesterday. Ken was reading the newspaper, drinking his hot and steamy cup of coffee; I was deciding whether to wear the black, short-sleeve T-shirt with slacks or the white, short-sleeve T-shirt with slacks. I chose the white. I walked out onto our porch, where Ken seemed so calm and peaceful, stood there with my hands planted ever so firmly on my hips, and said—or rather *announced* with great determination—that yes, I'd decided . . . "I want to foster a child." Ken nodded, continued reading the sports page, and as he sipped his coffee caught a glimpse of me over the rim of the cup. "Seriously, Ken, I want to be a mother." This was a conversation continuing from the night before.

Let me backtrack for just a moment. When Ken and I first met, there were two things that Ken never, ever wanted to do again: one was to get married and the other was to have a child. He had done both, and that was quite enough for him. I, too, felt when we met that marriage was a very iffy commitment. I mean, why? So that when you divorce, all the shit that was yours to begin with now has to get tossed into a legal heap, and maybe you won't get the CDs and those few pieces of furniture you brought to the marriage? But a few months after our first date, along with the I'm-never-getting-married-again lecture, we found ourselves picking out wedding rings and meeting with Unitarian ministers. We chose both within a week.

But I digress.

I had this urge, not necessarily to give birth but to fill an unyielding emptiness. I am not—I repeat, *not*—a nurturing woman in the *mothering* sense. I am very aware of my limitations. But I had this need, this urge, this flu-like symptom that would not go away. I thought that instead of adopting a child, we could, for lack of a better word, *rent* one. See if it works. I had heard both very good and very awful stories about foster care and fostering children. I knew a couple who brought a foster child into their home, and two weeks later felt they were being emotionally tortured. I have friends who had huge success at fostering a little girl and ended up adopting her, and another friend whose child turned out to be the devil doll. But I understood that these children needed to be loved. They needed to be cared for. Their place in the world was so fragile, so tentative, so very scary.

And I, obviously, had an urge: I needed to fill this empty space.

I stood there and waited for Ken to give me his blessing.

"Sure, fine. You wanna do this, go check it out."

"Wanna come with me?"

"Nah. I'm gonna watch football."

Ken later told me that, right or wrong, choosing a foster child was like going to the Bideawee pet rescue center or the humane society. This isn't something Ken cares to do, even though he is a very altruistic, kind, loving man. I was going to the Children's Aid Center to discuss the possibility of the two of us becoming foster parents and, while highly unlikely, maybe coming home with a happy, loving child with whom Ken could garden. Or at the very least, they could watch football together. I am such an optimistic fool.

I go to the Children's Aid office in our very small town. I am greeted with both a lack of enthusiasm and much paperwork— reams and reams of paperwork. I fill out most, call Ken twice (for his social security number, which I couldn't for the life of me remember, along with some financial information), and then I'm led to a small, empty room with a scattering of very old magazines. (I believe that any and all public spaces should keep up-to-date magazines—this is a cause I will champion in the future. There is nothing worse than old, old news.)

A young woman comes into the office. I can't tell if she's
Mormon or Amish. She's wearing a long, ankle-length, floral
schmata and a very, very bad haircut. Actually—truthfully—it looks
like a very bad helmet. She says nothing but gestures for me to follow her. As I walk out of the room behind her, I casually mention
that they ought to get some new *People* magazines.

I am now led to another room where the Mormon-slash-Amish
woman has a desk. I sit across from her and look around the room
for signs, clues of a life—her life. I see not one photo or calendar or
any other sign of life, period. In the corner, on the radiator, is what
appears to be a dead plant. I convince myself that that could happen
to anyone—not everyone has a green thumb.

She pulls out what appears to be a thick binder, slides it across
the desk, and motions for me to open it. I am now beginning to
think that maybe she is mute, since not a word has been spoken.
Perhaps, when speaking, I should move my lips very slowly, so she
can read them. I think this as I open the binder. There, in vivid color,
are snapshots, photos, eight-by-ten glossies of babies, young adults,
toddlers, and teenagers—black, white, Hispanic, Asian, mentally
disabled, physically challenged, older, taller. All in all, thirty to forty
photos. Some literally take my breath away. Melt my heart. A spar-
kle in the eyes; a dimple in the cheek; a turned-up nose; freckles;
thick, curly hair; missing teeth; a lazy eye; gorgeous skin tone. The
sadness is palpable. The joy, diminished. The desperation, obvious.

Then she speaks. She tells me it's a fairly long and complicated
process—that it could take weeks and weeks, maybe even a month
or two. Yes, yes, bureaucratic-bullshit paperwork (my words, not
hers). She doesn't like that I use the word *bullshit*, I can tell. She
continues, telling me how a lot of these kids are in homes and are
soon to be removed, or have to leave. I ask why. She says, "Well, it
didn't work out; there was a clash; the kids, you know, have issues.
Major, major issues. The foster parents have issues. Major, major

issues. Sometimes there's no patience or tolerance. Sometimes there are altercations. But they're getting filled up, and pretty soon these kids are going to be back to square one." Her words.

I stare out the window and think of Ken. He's probably soaking in a tub, bubble bath and all, watching his beloved New York Giants, screaming at the TV set, drinking a beer or a glass of Pinot Noir, and enjoying his life completely. Not a care in the world. He likes it that way.

•————•

I'd woken up days earlier, wanting to have a kid. I was hormonal and lonely and feeling depleted—spiritually lost. Hormonal, lonely, and lost, and older than the day before. Not a great combo. "I want a kid," I'd said, stamping my feet. Instead of going to the Woodbury Common outlet stores, I went to child services. Instead of trying on a pair of shoes, I looked through a binder of children who needed love, a home, and a place that was safe and kind, and who had probably never owned a pair of new shoes, because chances are their shoes were all hand-me-downs.

And that's when it all came together: the words *hand-me-downs*. I wasn't making a commitment to giving them a life or a future. I was teetering on making a decision to give them a place to live for a month or two, or maybe less. In my mind, they were returnable.

I felt so profoundly sad—heartbreakingly sad. I didn't want a child for the rest of his or her life; I wanted a child to take away my loneliness, my emptiness . . . for a month or two. And then it dawned on me in that empty, lifeless office, seated across from a woman who desperately needed a good haircut and a makeover, that I was being completely and utterly selfish.

I told the Amish-slash-Mormon woman that I needed some time to think about all of this. I couldn't be completely truthful with her and tell her that I had in fact wasted her time, because that would seem even more selfish. She asked me if I wanted to bring the binder home for my husband to look at the photos. I told her no, and she asked, "Does he like catalogs? Because this is just like flipping though a catalog."

In that moment, I stopped feeling selfish. I looked at her and said, "These kids, in this catalog—they need love; they need care. They need shoes. They're not pieces of clothing you pick out, thinking, *Well, if they don't fit, I can return them.* The children on these pages in this binder were not wanted when they came into the world, but they are not returnable. Your job is to find them a home. A loving home."

She looked at me, and her eyes, already filled with sadness, filled up with tears.

"I don't like my job," she said. "It's just that I feel so empty."

We were the same woman in that moment (except I had the better haircut).

"Hey, listen," I said. "I don't really want a kid. I want to fill a void, and I know what it's like to feel empty. I do, but while you're working here, at the very least, please, oh, please, when you hand the person or the couple the binder, please tell them that the pages are filled with huge potential and an amazing opportunity to love better, love more, and if you don't wanna do that, maybe you should quit your job and find something you love to do."

I hit a nerve, I could tell. I hugged her good-bye—a good strong hug. I told her that she should live her life out loud; that everyone—*everyone*—is scared, including me, and that I was very, *very* scared; that she should find the thing she loves to do and then do it. And although I thought it, I did not say, "Please, *I'm begging,* go out and get a good haircut." What I did say was, "Please, please, get rid of the dead plant. It's not inspiring."

And then it washed over me: the moment of absolute clarity. Sitting in my car at the light, waiting for it to change, clarity filled me to the brim. I didn't go to Children's Aid to foster a child; I went there to foster my very own spirit. To awaken to my very own life, to live more fully, to love myself better—to love better, period; to stop being so fucking selfish. To have enough faith in myself that I can stop thinking I have to—in this moment, right now, this very second—fill that void.

Ah.

Yes.

Jesus: A Love Story

Sylvie Simmons

A *long time ago and a long way away, I found Jesus. I was a little girl living in London, and Jesus lived in a cellar under the church at the end of our road. I would go and see him often, usually at night—crawl through the tumble of bushes along the sidewall and find the secret door that opened into a small, dark room smelling of damp and earth. After a few steps the floor became a sharp decline—a steep, flat surface on which I would lie, hands together, eyes closed, and slide down into a vast white cavern of a room. And that's where he would be waiting with his arms open: Jesus, whom I loved with all my heart.*

•————•

Saint Paul's was High Anglican—the peacock of the Church of England—with the kind of ceremonies and sacraments that, to the untrained eye, might look more Catholic than Protestant. My parents were Church of England insofar as this was the box they would tick if they were in hospital to have an operation. They did not go to church, though hardly anyone I knew in London did (except for weddings, christenings, and funerals). But once a week, my brothers and I went to Sunday school at Saint Paul's, which my parents picked because it was close enough to walk to on our own, giving them more time to do what parents do on a Sunday morning when the kids are gone. (This practical approach to religion seems to have run in my family. My grandmother, for example, Church of England and the widow of a Jew, joined the local Baptist church on the grounds of it having the best rummage sales.)

I loved Jesus, but I did not like the church. The vicar was impatient and never smiled. He would talk to us from behind a wooden lectern carved in the form of a griffin and, for emphasis, strike his hand down hard, over and over, on the book stand, which was the griffin's head. "Jesus loves the little children"—*whack!* I flinched at every blow; I knew what it was like to be beaten. I would picture the griffin finally having enough and rising up to rip the vicar limb from limb. (Not very Christian.) I did not like that vicar and I didn't need him to tell me that Jesus loved me. I knew he did. Though not as much as I loved him. I hadn't much experience of affection, but my heart almost burst with love for Jesus. I couldn't bear to look at the Cross: the nails in his hands and the wound in his side would move me to tears. My favorite image was the one in the *Children's Book of Bible Stories*: Jesus in a white robe, riding sidesaddle on a donkey up a cobbled hill, where white houses leaned against a solid blue sky. I loved this picture, although I knew it wasn't real. The sky, I knew, was grey, and buildings were black with soot and grime. And Jesus wasn't on a donkey on a hill, he was right there under my feet.

Yes, I knew about Heaven and Hell. I'd been taught that the Devil was "down below," with the bad people, and that Jesus was up there, sitting at the right hand of God the Father Almighty, from whence he shall come to judge the quick and the dead. But those were just words, like the picture in the Sunday-school book was just a drawing. They did nothing to affect my belief, which was also my reality—I guess you could call it my Faith, except that Faith is the evidence of things unseen, and I could see Jesus—that he was in the basement. Which didn't seem odd to me, since my family lived in a basement too. That it was a secret place held no difficulties, either; children are drawn to secrets. They're also drawn to rites and mystical ceremonies, like the ones I'd perform in bed underneath the sheet before I opened the door and fell into his arms in that deep unconscious place between wakefulness and sleep. My nighttime visits to Jesus were, I suppose, a recurring dream of sorts. I had several different recurring dreams during my childhood.

I can't remember details of what went on between us. I know there were only ever the two of us: my infantine religion had nothing inclusive or self-transcending about it; he was my own personal Jesus. I'm sure I must have done most of the talking and, knowing me, did so in the heightened language of prayer; I knew countless hymns and long passages from the Bible by heart. Jesus was kind and patient; he understood me—I knew that. And I remember exactly how he looked, the sentimental blond Jesus favored by Victorian and early twentieth-century British illustrators: long hair, short beard, sharp cheekbones, and faraway eyes. I also recall his brightness. He glowed. His radiance lit up the white room like a great ball of sun, and it warmed me up inside and filled me. For as long as I was with him, there was no more emptiness or hurt. It was comforting. But more than that, although I couldn't have explained it at the time, it was a kind of confirmation—that I was not in this alone. That suffering was not unique to me. That people had suffered since the world began; it's only the details that change.

Ah, change. I've thought long and hard, but I honestly don't know why and how things changed between us. Perhaps I outgrew him, like you do an imaginary friend. When I was eleven, my family moved to another part of London. I no longer went to Sunday school. And I had found a new love: the Beatles. It seemed to be a requirement that one had a favorite Beatle, and mine was John. I heard an anger and a tear in Lennon's voice that moved me greatly. This was a man who knew about suffering and pain. Kneeling on my Beatles rug, I would cut out photos of John from magazines and paste them in my hymnbook. He was my first pop idol, and I worshipped him.

Lennon was notorious for saying that the Beatles were more popular than Jesus. (The lesser-known end of the quote is "Jesus was all right, but his disciples were thick and ordinary; it's them twisting it that ruins it for me," a sentence I would come to relate to more as I grew up.) I'd never compared the Beatles and Jesus (at least not consciously), but pop music did seem somehow to offer greater hope. I was a romantic little girl and, without any good reason, an optimist, and for half my young life, I had been true to Jesus, pious and dutiful. But my life was no happier. To keep on keeping faith with just a promise of happiness at an unimaginable time takes some doing, and I was no Job. Cynicism had crept in.

So had hormones. Within a few years I was all flesh and estrogen. By the time I entered my teens, pop music had given way to rock—and with it sex and drugs, and so many good reasons to rebel. At the same time, the musicians began to look just like Jesus. If you were in London in the late sixties and went to a rock concert, you might well have run into the young blond man with the pale face and melancholy eyes wandering among the crowds in a long white robe, telling us his name was Jesus. Many of my own boyfriends, I have to say, would not have looked out of place on a cross. I had not thought of Jesus in that way, at least not consciously, as a boyfriend, someone I was sexually attracted to. But it might have been a clue into our breakup.

Jesus wasn't putting out; he was not that into me. He thought of me as a child. He was part of the old contract. The kind of love he offered wasn't liberating; it was a ball and chain. Anyway, it was over.

And so began the years of music, men, and mind-altering substances—my new obsessions to which I devoted myself with dedication. Between them, on a good day, they might take me out of myself for a while, transport me into another state of consciousness, or offer some taste of surrender or belonging or meaning or communion or peace or love. My religious impulse (or what was left of it) got an occasional and superficial workout during my adolescence—dipping a toe in Eastern mysticism, meditation, Khalil Gibran (the teenage pantheon of the time), mostly because they came recommended by rock stars or some other sad-eyed, young person with whom I shared a joint.

The Scientologists had managed to round up a posse of such people in London, who lingered outside the store on Tottenham Court Road and lured you in for a free engram test. The meter merely confirmed that I was as lost as I knew I was, so I didn't sign up for more. One time I found myself at a Mormon service. Two young-looking elders going door-to-door knocked on mine as I was drifting down from acid and told me they saw Jesus standing behind me in a ray of light on the stairs. When I looked around, he was gone. I let them take me to a place where some happy-looking people gave me a soft drink and showed me a film. They offered to baptize me then and there; I declined.

But I became a real and ardent church lover. I would go into churches all the time, though not for a Sunday service and not for Jesus or God, but for music and art. I loved (and still love) the paintings and sculptures, the stained-glass windows, the high, vaulted ceilings, and the graveyards with toppled stones. And I adored church music—all church music: organs, monastic chants, choirs, the simplicity and depth of the old hymns I grew up on. One afternoon, when

I dropped into a church in London, I saw an organ player practicing. We talked and he asked if I had ever seen a pipe room. I hadn't. He led me past the huge fan that cooled the pump and into a forest of enormous wooden pipes, then set me in the middle, which is where I stood while he played Bach with all the stops out. It was impossibly, gloriously loud. My whole body vibrated with the music. It was a deeply moving experience, but it did not bring me nearer to Jesus. I had come back to the church but as a tourist. The organ, the icons, the candles, the special silence were the sights and smells and sounds of my heritage—but also of my exile.

The distance between us widened when I moved to the United States to be a rock writer. I'd left England with a head full of American books, movies, and songs and believed, with the arrogance of youth, that I knew America. One very big culture shock was the relationship between Americans and the church. Same God, same hymns, same Jesus on the Cross, but that's about where it ended. The United States had literal belief and politics; the United Kingdom had Monty Python's *Life of Brian* and the Queen. Americans seemed to pray like everyone was watching; in Britain, the Church was rarely discussed and barely thought about. There was no one on TV trading prayers for pounds, no mobs outside Westminster Abbey when a new Archbishop of Canterbury was named. The Church of England, like the Queen who headed it (as all monarchs have since Henry VIII parted with Rome over his love life), was—at least for people of a certain generation and background—simply *there*. In America I felt the need to take sides. I lost all desire to visit a church.

In the decades that followed, if Transcendence or Grace or a Higher Power crossed my mind, I can't say I remember. Music and words were what kept me going. Even if I hadn't done it for a living, they were the medium in which I examined sin and redemption, heart and soul, beauty and pain. Though (the Devil is in the details) I can't recall having ever thought about it that way at the time. I was in the center of an exciting storm, going from escapade to escapade and deadline to deadline with a community of fellow thinkers, writers, and musicians—but for the most part working on my own. A wonderful distraction from old wounds that wouldn't heal, but there were new ones—deep ones—too.

I did not call on Jesus for help and comfort. Having moved back to England, then France, I did renew my passion for churches and their objects of metal, glass, and wood, but I was never able to imbue them with life. There were times I desperately wanted to—times when things happen that pull the world out from under you, emptiness swallows you, and nothing makes any sense. Death and despair have a way of turning a mind to religion, and for a while I tried, I prayed, I went to church alone and lit candles, gazed at the Cross (which can still make me cry), and tried to summon a vision of a happy afterlife. I faked it basically—faked what I could not feel in the hope that, if I kept at it long enough, the feeling would come back on its own.

Is there a Viagra for Faith? A medical solution? Although I'm back living in America, where religion and reason seem even more set at opposite corners in a fight to the death, I still might volunteer. I seem to have met more seekers than ever—countless people poring through self-help books, going to meditation classes, chanting, breathing, or wandering like refugees looking for a spiritual home, *any* home, whether one's own or adopted. On the dresser I have a statuette of a plump and happy man staring at the hands in his lap; on the piano there's a man with his arms nailed to a cross, calling to the sky in agony: "O God, why hast thou forsaken me?"

I miss Jesus—I admit it. On a recent trip to London, I went back to Saint Paul's. He didn't seem to be there.

If There Is a God, Why Would S(He) Waste All Her Time Making Hell?

Pam Houston

> Faith does not need to push the river
> because faith is able to trust that there is a river.
> The river is flowing. We are in it.
> —Richard Rohr

I hate the holidays. Let's start with that—the period each year from Halloween all the way through Christmas and New Year's, and on to my birthday in early January. I am, generally speaking, a reasonably happy, optimistic person (albeit with a slight New Jersey edge), but the holidays are a vortex. A black, light-sucking hole, a dying red giant of a season.

I should say up front that I don't blame God in the least for my feelings or even for Christmas itself, which in its contemporary version S(He) could not possibly approve of. I have no good excuse for my feelings, except that a lot of bad shit happened in my family of origin, and either more of it happened around the holidays, or it was during the holiday season when I realized, because of the families on TV commercials, exactly how bad my family's shit was. And

while I understand now that those commercials are fake and that
the trifecta of abuse that went on in my family was as common in
suburbia as Hamburger Helper, and while very good therapy and a
life dedicated to the making of art has fixed me in so many ways
(just ask my therapist), nothing mitigates the terror leading up to
Halloween, nor the two months of taking the small, measured breaths
that follow.

Before the internet, it was possible to spend the holiday season
in countries where they didn't actually know it was Christmas, and
I could usually convince some magazine or other to send me there.
That option is now defunct, however, so I employ other strategies.
I have volunteered at soup kitchens, gone solo camping in the desert,
tasked myself with picking the perfect present for every single person I know, burrowed in at the ranch with a 750-page novel, skied
every day until my legs turned to rubber, and spent whole long eve-
nings staring into my Irish wolfhound's eyes. All of these strategies
are marginally effective, and I have gained confidence over the years
in my ability to power through.

This year, my stepdaughter's mother's marriage ended just
before Thanksgiving, so I dropped it into 4-wheel low and became
Mrs. Fucking Claus on Kaeleigh's behalf. I did the wreath, the roast,
the stockings hung by the chimney with care, the cookies in the shapes
of reindeer, trees, and bells (and, oddly, something that resembled a
buffalo); we sewed popcorn and cranberries onto a string.

Because none of us wanted to kill a tree, but we liked the idea
of plastic even less, we skied out to the back of the property and
cut boughs from the bottom of one of the giant Colorado spruce
trees, brought them back on a sled, and screwed them to two two-
by-eights, creating a tree as beautiful as any TV commercial and that
no living thing had to die for. I even dug out a CD from the Pottery
Barn called *A Cool Christmas*, evidently purchased the last time I
impersonated someone who can actually do the holidays.

We made a candy gingerbread house. We watched *Love, Actually* twice. We, by God, out-Christmased Christmas at the ranch this year, and on New Year's Eve we watched the ball come down like any good American citizens. To put it another way, I overcame my substantial limitations to do right by Kaeleigh, and when it was all over, I didn't feel so much self-congratulatory as I felt like I had been through one of those Billy Jack–type rituals, where you get bitten by a rattlesnake a thousand times so you will be reborn as a person who never fears snakes again.

I only go into all this so you will understand my frame of mind on January 5, 2014, as I descended in a plane over Orlando, Florida, the whole shebang behind me, with thirty-six hours all to myself before I had anywhere to be. Grateful as I am—and I *am*—that I'm finally well enough to have made a longish-term (seven years and counting), family-type relationship work with not one but *two* other human beings, what I miss most from my old, dysfunctional life is alone time. I am an only child of abusive alcoholics, and no matter what my brain knows, my body still remembers. When I am alone, I believe I am safe and happy and free.

It was all I could do not to dance among the mouse-eared throngs at the airport. Outside, it was warm and humid, and the air felt gentle all around me. In a rented Chevy Malibu, so saturated with pot smoke that I got a contact high every time the sun emerged from a cloud and hit the windshield, I drove straight to New Smyrna Beach and the Atlantic Center for the Arts (ACA), where in thirty-six hours, I would meet the students in my week-long writing class.

I know Florida is not without its corruptions, but there is something about it that makes me so damn happy. I love New Smyrna in particular for its throwback approach to beach life and for the ACA, which is exactly what paradise would look like if paradise were designed by a committee of artists—a compound of studios (dance, painting, writing, sculpture) hidden deep in the palmetto forest, each building more architecturally spectacular than the last, linked by a boardwalk under which armadillos and the occasional alligator scurry. I also love New Smyrna for its proximity to the quiet end of Canaveral National Seashore, and for JB's Fish Camp, where you can get a dozen oysters for what three cost in California, or blackened grouper with a side of corn on the cob, and eat it right on the dock, where every once in a while a manatee shows up to see what's happening.

When I got to the ocean, the gentle breeze of Orlando had turned into a wind so stiff it was hard to walk against; the Atlantic more resembled the Pacific, that misnamed ocean, all churned up with big sets coming in sideways. I tried it for a while, because how many people get to walk on the beach in January? But eventually I gave up and went to JB's to watch playoff football, eat oysters, and drink a Dark and Stormy at the bar.

•———•

For the last fifteen years, I have taught creative writing in an English department with a bunch of people who think that to believe in anything makes you moronic, even if it's echinacea, even if it's dogs. They are, when taken as a group, the most intellectually gifted and most spiritually limited people I have ever known. Their atheism, in my experience of it, is precisely as rigid as a militant Christian's belief that the recent rash of extreme weather events are the punishment God has exacted upon us because S(He) doesn't like homosexuals. What amazes me is not their lack of belief in God—a lot of my friends don't believe in God—but their degree of certainty about it.

I don't understand how anyone with a 150-plus IQ and the most basic understanding of human history can be 100 percent sure about anything. We were wrong about the shape of the earth, and we were wrong about the continents being fixed upon it. We were wrong about the four humors of human physiology, and we were wrong about the static nature of the Universe. We were wrong about DDT and thalido-mide and margarine. We are in the process of realizing we are wrong about backscatter airport security and those energy-saving light bulbs, which are full of mercury that, even the EPA admits, when broken, are in danger of toxifying our homes.

What would be the odds that in 2014 we would have finally under-stood everything correctly and completely, that our brains would have finally enlarged to the point where we know all there is to know? It strikes me as both braver and more hopeful to believe that there are facets to the world that our brains will never be even on the verge of understanding, wonders that make our finest measuring tools obso-lete. It also strikes me as a lot more fun.

• ———— •

The next morning it was still blowing hard, but the sun was out so I tried the beach again. At Canaveral, the only people willing to brave the wind and big surf were the pompano fishermen. There was a clus-ter of them at the end of each of the walkways that traverse the dunes from the five parking lots that spread themselves along the length of the barrier island. The sea was so violent that, in places, the waves crashed all the way up to the high dunes. Walking promised to be difficult at best—and dangerous at worst—but this was my only day off, so I left the car in Lot 4 and headed south. Sometimes I had a foot or two of sand to walk on between the water and the base of the dune. But sometimes the waves ripped right up underneath me, soaking my shorts, and I had to dig my toes in—once even dig my hands in—to keep from getting swept out to sea.

A misty marine layer hung over the beach, and before long I was out of sight of the fishermen. The biggest wave so far came in, knocking me to one knee, and I was just beginning to entertain the idea that what I was doing might actually be stupid when I saw, ahead of me, indistinct in the mist, a man in a full-size lawn chair perched up on the edge of the dune. My first thought was, *It seems like a long way to have dragged that chair*. My second was, *Oh, he's naked*.

Some of my Colorado friends—the ones who were not born in New Jersey—think that every time they hit the East Coast they are in danger of getting caught up in an episode of *The Sopranos*, and I was determined not to make the same error. Something about the way the naked man held his body while tanning, combined with his purple doo-rag, suggested I had nothing to fear. I could see a half mile in either direction, and there was not another soul in sight. I kept my eyes on the crescent of beach and continued walking. He said nothing and I said nothing, and soon I was alone again.

Then I saw the trash bag tossed up into the palmettos with something heavy and awkward straining the sides. Human limbs jumped immediately to mind, speaking of *The Sopranos*. I stopped and stared at the bag a minute before deciding that nothing good could possibly come from my looking inside. Even if it were a person, my opening the bag was not going to help them reattach their limbs—to say nothing of the fact that it would ruin my one perfect day, during which I was bound to nothing and no one.

I walked on, my heart beating a little faster. No sign of anybody, and more surprisingly, no sign of the next boardwalk that led to Lot 5. Lots 1–4 had been, I thought, at one-mile intervals, but even with the waves impeding my progress, I knew I'd walked more than a mile. The beach and wild dunes were heart-stoppingly beautiful— the ocean still a happy, frothy chaos—and yet there was no denying that the mist, the naked man, the bag, and the disappearance of Lot 5 were lending a distinctly *Twilight Zone* feel to the morning. I wondered if it had been a mistake to leave my cell phone behind.

•———————•

Religion gets a bad name in the circles I run in, largely because so many people try to employ it in the name of rectitude. I could never believe in a punishing God, because we do such a great job of punishing ourselves and each other; a punishing God would be redundant. I could never believe in a judgmental God or an exclusive God, or a God who would even prefer one outcome over another. Because of everything I learned during my time in Asia, my God has more than a little of the Buddha thrown in.

I can't believe in a God who will help me win the lottery or one who will keep me from getting cancer. But I can believe in one who will help see me through if either of those things should happen. I can believe in a God who will teach me generosity—one who has made me understand that generosity is its own reward.

When I write first drafts, I have always tended to erroneously capitalize nouns that stand for some of my favorite things: Ocean, Elk, Sushi, Wolfhound. It has become no small source of amusement for my editor, but I think I must be subconsciously honoring the things in the world that I find holy. In my Universe, I am coming to understand all those capitalized nouns equal God.

•———————•

I walked another hundred yards or so before the beach narrowed and steepened slightly. My uphill hip started to ache, so I tried walking across the top of the dunes for a while before I realized this was both ecologically irresponsible and harder still. I descended and continued to sidehill as I tried to decide whether to continue my quest for the elusive Lot 5 or turn back and retrace my steps. I thought when I arrived that the tide couldn't get any higher, but it did not seem to be in any hurry to go out. Another giant wave pounded onto the beach, shooting up my legs, this time soaking my shirt all the way to my bra line. It was at that moment when I realized I was no longer holding the rent-a-car key in my hand.

And then, on the other side of the coin, are all those who have dedicated their lives to trying to prove God's existence, a task that seems
fundamentally misguided to me. If we had proof, we wouldn't need
faith, and I'd hate to lose faith because faith's the best part. Faith gives
us the opportunity to take action in the face of uncertainty—in the
face of our most undeniable, most difficult truth, which is exactly
what all the most valuable things ask of us. Art, for example, and love.

I believe in mystical experiences because I have had some.
I believe in a benevolent presence because I can't explain many
things—including the world's bright beauty—without one. I have,
for the purposes of this essay, called that presence God, though I am
not attached to the word itself and would just as comfortably use
another. I would never attempt to force my beliefs onto others nor
attempt to make my version of faith match anyone else's. For faith to
be worth anything at all to me, it has to be a chaotic, uncertain, and
ungovernable thing.

•———————•

Now my heart was really pounding. I had to have had the key in my
hand when I left the car, because I remembered it beeping, remembered double-checking, because of the signs about valuables posted
around the parking lot. If I dropped it immediately, it might still be
next to the car, although there was a better chance someone would
have seen it, would have taken the pot-scented Malibu (or at least
the iPhone and credit card inside it) for a joy ride. More likely, I
dropped it along the way, when I was worried about a wave or the
naked man or the body bag, or just feeling too damn good about
the fact that no one on the face of the earth knew where I was—so
excited was I about my day, which I worried was about to turn into
something completely different.

I turned around and, as best I could, followed the ghost
imprints of my tracks back toward Lot 4. I wasn't sure exactly

what I would do when I got there. Even if the car were still parked, I had no phone, no money, no identification. It was, I thought, exactly like the old days, when I would have befriended an elderly couple in the parking lot who would have taken me to a pay phone, where I could ask the operator to call the 1-800 number for Hertz. Were there still pay phones in Florida? If so, were there actual operators on the other end? Perhaps I could find that same elderly couple and ask them to take me to JB's, where the bartender might remember me (we'd had a nice football chat) and let me use their phone to call ACA, where someone might answer, even though it was the weekend.

Something good would probably come of this, I tried to tell myself, though the tide seemed even higher than before. And I noticed, for the first time, that my mouth was very dry, and among the things I had left in the car was water. I hurried, without knowing exactly why. I passed the body bag. I passed the naked man. Full frontal in this direction, but now that I had a bigger problem than any I could imagine him causing me, I gave him a smile and a nod. An hour had gone by since I realized I wasn't holding the key.

Every once in a while my tracks reappeared for a moment, five or eight or ten footprints at a time emerging and then disappearing for a hundred yards, where the ocean had washed the beach completely clean. I was in such a patch of six or eight footsteps, nearly back in sight of the pompano fishermen, when I saw the plastic Hertz key chain and the black electronic key lying, untouched and dry, on the sand. I picked it up. I read the words *Gold Chevy Malibu*. They could not have been anyone else's keys—and yet I was so amazed that they had been returned to me that I imagined, for a minute, some other Gold Chevy Malibu in the parking lot. I sat down in the patch of relatively dry sand where the key had been and laughed.

"Thank you," I said, out loud, to the sky.

I can't explain exactly why I believed, the second I saw the key lying on that tiny patch of dry sand, that God had something to do with it. Especially since I did not believe, or at least was not willing to say—even to myself—that God had anything to do with the time I did not drown in Cataract Canyon when my boat flipped in Big Drop #2 during the hundred-year flood and I had to ride into the gaping maw of Big Drop #3 in just my life jacket, a five-gallon water cooler stuffed between my legs. I was not willing to say that God had any-thing to do with the time I did not get knifed by the kid who wanted my sleeping bag on Andros Island, Bahamas, when he found me sleeping in it behind the town's electricity generator. This was after I'd talked my way onto a cargo plane from Fort Lauderdale and was subsequently being pursued by Bahamian customs officials. I had a MailBoat to catch in an hour, I told the boy with the knife, rubbing sleep from my eyes, or the customs guys were going to catch up with me, and I needed to keep my sleeping bag for myself, because I never knew where I'd be spending the night. (I know that story smells like drug running, but it was really only extremely low-budget adventure.)

I likewise failed to give God credit when I was not eaten by the fifteen-foot hammerhead shark who cast his big shadow over me when I was swimming in thirty feet of Caribbean water, a bloody grouper in one hand and a spear gun in the other, or when I didn't lose my legs when a female grand caiman, nearly the size of the shark, jumped into the front of my dugout canoe because the river guide—as a joke—was making the distress sounds of a baby grand caiman. And this list doesn't scratch the surface of near misses, which includes the four times I have been told to get into crash position on a commercial airliner, or the forty-eight hours I spent surviving Hurricane Gordon in a fifty-two-foot Irwin with torn sails and a hit-or-miss motor, or the night I managed to keep my skis on top of the leading edge of an avalanche on a full-moon run down Berthoud Pass. Not to mention my father's violence (he broke my femur when

I was four), or both my parents' drinking (I walked or was pulled from sixteen totaled vehicles before my sixteenth birthday).

And yet, it is only now, just starting down the far side of fifty, that this phrase begins beating like a drum in my head: *I have always been looked after.*

I have always been looked after, says the drum, over and over, like the way I learned that if I didn't fight it, my body would always come to the surface of the water; like a song my mother might have sung to me (if she had ever sung to me)—a thing, like breathing, that now that I know, I can't unknow—a thing, I realize now, I have always known, though I wasn't able, in the past, to call it God. Even now, the word seems limited, a little misused, and frankly, a little too short to mean everything I feel when I look, for example, at the mercuried surface of a river in twilight and know that in some way I may not ever be capable of grasping that everything is going to be okay.

Like everything worth having—like the best kind of art and the best kind of love—faith snuck up on me slowly, until one day I heard myself saying the word God unapologetically, until it started to roll off my tongue like Ocean and Elk and Sushi and Wolfhound—all the things I love in this deeply lovable world.

• ——— •

This story is unspectacular; I know that. Even if my car key had gone out to sea, somebody in Lot 4 would have helped me, and Hertz would have forgiven me; I would have made it back to ACA in time to teach my class. The only thing that would have been compromised was this one perfect day, which as it happened, included a swim, when the tide finally went out and the ocean settled down, followed by a late afternoon snack of a dozen more oysters at JB's.

"I had the best day ever," I told my class that night, when we gathered in the writing studio, which I might have said even if my key had wound up at the bottom of Davy Jones's locker (but against a hundred-to-one odds it did not).

It is also not a conversion story. It will convince not one of my colleagues at UC Davis, nor probably any other people, that God exists or that S(He) is on our side. It's just a story of a day when I realized my reality had expanded a little in one sweet and soulful direction. I laughed in the sand when I found that key, and I laugh again now as I write about it, and that makes me think laughter is at least one of the responses God is looking for. Maybe S(He) gets a kick out of doing a party trick now and then for kids who didn't get to go to too many parties. Maybe, for reasons I'll never understand, S(He) wanted me to have a really good day.

III

We've all lost someone we loved. Whenever I've been faced with grief and the challenge of accepting loss, I've thought of friends whose faith supports and comforts. Although I feel a profound faith in the potential goodness of humanity, I often wish I could add to that an equally profound faith in God. The idea of never feeling alone is so powerful, and those who believe in God share that nurturing conviction. I not only envy them, I hope to perhaps one day join them, but my journey is just beginning, and I'm still at that place where I'm asking myself, *Will I ever believe in something with such certainty that it would sustain me not only through moments of loss and despair but through the everyday tableaux of life?* This is the question that forms in my brain and then tightens my chest, wrapping itself around my heart, refusing to release its hold. And yet, as I type the question, I have to smile, because while I struggle with the very concept of God, I have always been driven by an abiding belief—an abiding faith—in life and in the goodness of humanity. My glass is always half full (if not completely full!), and I've enjoyed a lifelong optimism reminding me that good will always conquer evil.

I teach creative nonfiction (personal essay) in the UCLA Extension Writers' Program, and occasionally discover a student whose writing skills are equal to those of many published authors. DeNae Powers Handy submitted a short essay on faith, and her words touched me. In this excerpt, she writes about how our beliefs shift with time and age:

> The God of my faith not only supports malleability of belief but encourages it to the degree that He provides the blueprints for change. I'm not surprised that as I move into midlife, my personal landscape requires flexibility and stability in equally increasing amounts. Some ideas I once considered certainties have been painted over by new truths, brushed into the picture by age and experience. But that canvas—faith that God has a plan designed just for me—remains fixed, even as the scenes that sweep across it expand in breadth, deepen in complexity, and brighten in love, hope, and joy.

Grace Happens

Barbara Graham

I have come to Germany to be saved.

Not from Satan in that Jesus-rapture-float-up-to-heaven sort of way; I have come to be saved from myself.

It might seem odd for a Jewish pilgrim from New York to be searching for salvation in Hadamar, the tiny village where Josef Mengele conducted his evil experiments half a century before, but this is the town where many devotees who travel to see Mother Meera stay.

Born in India in 1960 to farmers, Mother Meera was recognized to be an incarnation of the Divine Feminine when she was just eight years old. It is said that she was put on earth to help human beings prepare for transformation to a higher level of consciousness. In her book *Answers*, she explains that her purpose is "to help humans and to make them happy, peaceful, contented, harmonious, and loving."[1]

I want to be all of those things. More than anything I want to stop being afraid—of everything. Still, I'm not sure whether a person who is, confusingly, both a skeptic and a true believer (i.e., me) can be helped, but I'm hoping for a little grace.

I'm nervous and excited as our group from the hotel boards the shuttle bus that will take us to Thalheim, the nearby hamlet where Mother lives, and where four nights a week she offers *darshan*. Roughly translated from the Hindi, *darshan* means a meeting with a holy person.

It is a moonless, frigid evening in February. I am with my two best friends, Mark and Florence. As our bus bumps along the country road, I notice the actor Terence Stamp sitting up front, right behind the driver. I wonder if he, like me, has come to Germany hoping to experience bliss—or at the very least, relief from an endlessly spinning—and in my case, chronically terrified—monkey mind.

Many of my friends, including Mark and Florence, are seasoned veterans of *darshan* with Mother Meera. From them and others, I've heard reports of extraordinary states elicited by her presence: profound peace, exquisite joy, myriad visions, perfect love, showers of white light like a heavenly snowfall.

I am trying to tamp down my expectations. I've been around spiritual circles long enough to know that mystical fireworks aren't a prerequisite for happiness or even enlightenment. In fact, many sages warn that clinging to visions and experiences of bliss can get in the way of true freedom. Still, I yearn—I can't help it. I have serious issues with my own mother, which may help to explain why I long to be bathed in the unconditional love of the Divine Mother. I'm hoping that a little taste of the Divine will give me the confidence boost I need to start believing that I'm not broken. I hope, too, that the skeptic in me doesn't block the transmission of Divine Light.

"Stop worrying so much," Mark tells me. "Your experience will be whatever it is. You can't control it, so you might as well just let go."

"Ha!" I say. "If I knew how to let go, I probably wouldn't be here."

When our bus pulls up to Mother's house, I see about one hundred other pilgrims already assembled, waiting for the front door to open. We join them at the rear of the line. Again, I marvel that this gathering is taking place in a remote village that doesn't appear on most maps. In another way, though, maybe it's not so surprising that Mother Meera has chosen this spot; even now, in 1994, I imagine that Germany could use some spiritual healing. When the door finally opens, we file in, leaving our shoes and coats in an anteroom before entering the large main room and taking a seat. Once we're settled and sitting quietly, Mother Meera appears, and we stand until she takes her place at the front of the room. I am awed by my first glimpse of this woman—this purported emanation of the Divine Mother. In her purple and gold Sari, she looks like a queen.

Darshan, which lasts about two hours, is held entirely in silence. After a period of meditation, we approach Mother one by one. The ritual is precisely structured. When it's our turn, we do *pranam*. That is, we kneel and bow before Mother Meera, allowing her to hold our head in her hands. This lasts for about thirty seconds. As she explains in *Answers*, during *pranam* she is undoing invisible knots that are obstacles to our spiritual growth. When she releases our head, we gaze into her eyes for however long she gazes into ours. "I am looking at everything within you to see where I can help, where I can give healing and power," she says in the book. "At the same time I am giving Light to every part of your being, I am opening every part of yourself to Light."[2] This goes on for another twenty or thirty seconds—and sometimes less, as I will soon discover. Finally, when Mother Meera casts her eyes downward, she is signaling that our turn is over and she's ready to receive the next person.

I wish I could report that I felt a powerful current when Mother Meera held my head, or a blast of Divine Light when she looked into my eyes, but I did not. The experience was lovely in a simple, quiet sort of way, but I'd been hoping for more of a Big Bang effect and was disappointed.

"I think it's me," I say to Florence in our hotel room after my second uneventful *darshan*. "I really believe that amazing experiences happen—only to other people." This is another old belief I've come to Thalheim hoping to dispel: that profound joy and peace are available to every seeker on the planet except me.

"I think Mother Meera gives you what you need, which is not necessarily the same as what you want or what you think you want," Florence replies.

"Maybe." Besides, we're staying for twelve days, which means six more *darshans* to go. *Surely I will have some sort of transformative experience in the days to come*, I think before falling into a deep sleep, unaware of just how prescient Florence's words would prove to be.

• ———— •

For years I've aspired to undo the anxiety and fearfulness that seem hardwired into me. I've done everything I could think of to ease my tense body and galloping mind. Too often it feels as if my whole nervous system is rigged to remain on high alert, as if, at any moment, the Cossacks will burst through the door. I am banking on Mother Meera to help me break the cycle—for myself, as well as my son and his future children. This fear reflex feels somehow karmic, genetic, cellular, ancient, and—despite my efforts—completely outside of my control.

I come by it honestly. I grew up believing that if you worried hard enough, bad things wouldn't happen to you. This was the legacy passed on to me by my mother, my grandmother, and her mother before her—nervous women whose constant panic over every conceivable threat, from kidnappers and cancer to airplane crashes and the atom bomb, was supposed to act as a sort of inoculation (like the Salk vaccine) that would protect you from suffering and death. The idea was that if you paid your dues in terror, along with the ulcers and migraines that went with it, then you and your loved ones would be spared the full catastrophe.

Of course, this was all unspoken. To say such things aloud would be to break the spell. *Puh puh. Kaynahora.* Anyhow, there was no need; fear was transmitted directly through the DNA. There were plenty of reasons for this, including a long history of fleeing and persecution. As a girl of six, before her family immigrated to Pittsburgh from a *shtetl* in Russia, my grandmother was stoned by bands of roving Cossacks while playing near the river.

Judaism may have been our religion—we may have given lip service to God—but we put our faith in fear.

Still, by the time I reached high school, it had become pretty obvious that such magical thinking not only made you miserable, it didn't work. Three out of four of my anxious grandparents had died. So had my friend's fifteen-year-old sister, who had gone home from school one day with a sore throat and was stone-cold dead the next. Even my favorite uncle, whose wife was a world-class worrier, dropped dead of a heart attack at fifty-four. Although the evidence clearly demonstrated that fear could not outsmart death—and really, *all* fear is a defense against death and annihilation—I was caught in its grip. To my mind, every mosquito was a tsetse fly, and I instantly contracted every ailment I got wind of. Spinal meningitis when my classmate's sister died of it, a brain tumor when my kid cousin got diagnosed with one, yellow fever while reading *The Good Earth*. Plagued by panic attacks during college, I often rushed myself to the ER, convinced I was dying. When, at twenty-three, I became a mother, my FQ (fear quotient) hit the stratosphere. Now I didn't just

have myself to worry about, I had a baby who was dependent on me
to keep him safe. Like a trapped animal, I couldn't see my way out.
What calamity would befall me—or worse, my son—if I stopped
being afraid?

The word *faith* comes from the Latin *fide*—to trust. I had never
learned to trust in life. Still, the older I got, the more I wearied of
my anxiety, the more I hungered to break free. Despite—or perhaps,
because of—my conditioning, I longed to ignite an inner spark that
had also been with me since childhood: on some level I'd always
sensed that I was connected to something much greater than myself,
even though I had no name for it. It was this spark—dim but never
extinguished—that propelled me on a quest that took many turns
before I found myself in an unremarkable village in Germany,
kneeling at the feet of the Divine Mother.

·———·

"Life is suffering."

The first time I heard the Buddha's First Noble Truth was on
a rainy spring night in 1989. The speaker was Sogyal Rinpoche, a
highly regarded teacher of Tibetan Buddhism, and listening to him
talk, I began to weep. *So, it isn't just me*, I thought with enormous
relief. Sorrow and fear are built into the human condition: we're
born, we love, we create a life; then at some point, we and everyone
we've ever loved die. None of this was news, but Sogyal's words—
and the Buddha's teachings—cast a clear, impersonal light on my
suffering. I wasn't alone. Or pathological. This was just life, the
human story—insights I hadn't fully digested during years of individual therapy. That night, I felt as if I'd come home, spiritually
speaking.

But as profound and as simple as the First Noble Truth is, the next
three—which lead to the end of suffering—are where the real work
lies. If we are ever to be at peace, we must recognize that, in our igno-

rance, we're the sole source of our own unhappiness. It's our desire, in any given moment, for life to be different from the way it actually is that causes us to suffer. The Zen Buddhists call this gap between reality and our experience the difference between heaven and hell—which sums up the Second Noble Truth. But there is a way out: becoming aware that we're the source of our own suffering enables us to see that we're also the source of our own happiness, our own refuge— the Third Noble Truth. The Fourth, which some call enlightenment or nirvana, is the fruit—the end of suffering—in which we achieve the freedom of mind to see that we are already complete, seamlessly connected to all life, with nothing lacking in this present moment, even when this moment is difficult and shot through with fear.

It is a conundrum of Buddhist teachings that we're already whole and enlightened, yet in order to fully realize—or even catch a glimpse of—our true nature, we must cultivate the desire to do so by practicing meditation, grappling with impermanence, and following the Buddha's Eightfold Path, usually for many years—perhaps lifetimes. True, there are some who experience spontaneous awakenings with little or no effort, but I was not one of those people.

After hearing Sogyal Rinpoche speak, I dove headlong into the Buddhist world and sampled various traditions like someone trying on outfits, searching for the one best suited to me. I attended talks and empowerments, daylong events and longer retreats led by an assortment of Tibetan lamas, Zen masters, and Vipassana teachers. Many different flavors, same basic principles. I loved the Tibetan teachers, who were charming and delightful, but found the practices too arcane, too ornate. Zen was a little strict, Vipassana a little dry. I grew restless in my pursuit, restless in my meditation. Although I took solace from the teachings and being in the presence of remarkable teachers, including His Holiness the Dalai Lama, I was having trouble getting past the First Noble Truth. I still felt trapped inside a layer of fear that I couldn't seem to shake. I yearned for that inner spark to ignite and offer me a glimpse of something I couldn't name—some sign that there was hope for the likes of me.

And so, while I continued to practice meditation and explore the Buddhist path, I branched out. I didn't want to wait a lifetime (or three) to feel more at peace or one with the universe; I wanted results *now*. I felt then about healers and spiritual teachers the way I'd once felt about boyfriends before I met my husband: I longed to find The One. For a time I had a dalliance with the Jewish Renewal movement and got involved with a group affiliated with Reb Zalman Schachter-Shalomi. I was intrigued, but after a weekend retreat during which a bunch of us crawled around a dirty barn floor re-enacting the story of Jacob and Esau, my interest waned.

I moved on to astrologers, shamans, energy healers, clairvoyants, and a well-known past-life regression therapist under whose guidance I flashed on an image of myself as skeletal and half dead, riding naked in the back of a truck piled high with bodies, then being tossed like a sack of grain into a mass grave by Nazis. Whether this was a genuine memory or a scene served up by my unconscious mind, I'll never know. In any case, on some level it felt true, and I wept for days afterward. Still, the fear that seemed to be written in my body lingered.

So off to Germany I flew, hoping to shed my terror in the Divine Light of Mother Meera like a snake casting off its useless, old skin.

• ———— •

The night after my second ho-hum *darshan* I am awakened by a horrific nightmare. As with most of my nightmares (and daymares), it's about my son. In this one, I'm standing on a beach at the edge of thundering waves during a violent storm, watching helplessly—trying to scream but unable to utter a sound as my boy is carried out to sea.

Half-awake, I lie in the darkness trembling, drenched in sweat. My first thought is: *Why does everyone else who comes to see Mother*

Meera seem to have blissful, transcendent experiences, while I'm stuck in the shadow zone of my stubborn, fearful mind? My second thought is: *The fact that this nightmare occurred here is auspicious. Now, finally, I have the opportunity to relinquish my terror by turning it over to the Divine Mother, who, in my imaginings, will absorb it like a sponge, then neutralize it with her love, releasing me from its stranglehold.* What's more, my expectations are cosmic: *Not only will she free me from the legacy of fear that continues to hold me in its grip (and which I've passed on to my son like a bad gene), she'll free my son—and future generations—too.*

Although under ordinary circumstances I would have tried to dispel the heavy emotions that follow in the nightmare's wake, this time I cling to them. All day, I weep and wallow. I think it best to present Mother Meera with the full catastrophe so she can transform it on the spot.

That evening in *darshan* I'm silently tearful until, heart zinging around in my chest, I work up the courage to take my place before her. I am shaking as she holds my head during *pranam*, and I start to sob when she looks into my eyes. Then something shocking happens that I haven't witnessed with anyone else: instead of fixing me in her usual thirty-secondish gaze, she dismisses me almost immediately.

I feel devastated. Rejected. Rebuffed. Unseen. Crushed.

Not only were my emotions too much for my own mother to deal with, the Divine Mother can't seem to handle them either.

I feel like an outcast—a pariah among the holy. Marked.

Florence stays up half the night trying to console me.

"You can't take it personally," she says over and over. "Mother Meera does what she thinks is best for each person. Try to trust in that. Remember, she gives you what, in her greater wisdom, she senses you need most."

But I don't believe her. I don't believe I need rejection. I am beyond consolation.

The next five *darshans* are fine—even lovely—and I get as much time with Mother as anyone—but that single *darshan* stains my perception of the rest. I leave Thalheim feeling alone, defective, without the blessing or sense of freedom I long for.

My experience in Germany is a sort of spiritual riddle that takes me years to solve, years to grasp that, in fact, I did get what I needed most.

•————•

Shortly before his death, the Buddha told his grieving, brokenhearted disciples, who had been with him for forty years: "Be a lamp unto yourself, be a refuge to yourself. Look not for a refuge in anyone besides yourself."

I see now that by looking away so quickly, Mother Meera was returning to me the whole catastrophe that I had hoped to turn over to her—not because she couldn't handle my distress but because she wanted me to know that *I* could handle it. She saw that what I needed most was to take refuge in myself. To trust my own capacity to heal and wake up. The light she shone that night led me home to myself— that was her blessing, her gift that, for so long, felt like a curse.

At least that's what I believe, what rings most true.

In *Answers*, more than a decade later, I read: "There is no such thing as a bad darshan. To think so is wrong, harmful, and danger-ous. Darshan is completely impersonal from my side; I give what is needed . . . Try not to impose on me your difficulties and to project on me your own hidden problems. Have the courage to face your own weaknesses, and know that I am giving help continually."[3]

•————•

Fear may have been hardwired into my DNA, but it also provided me with a slant on life, an identity, a false sense of protection and control, a kind of armor that held me together while also holding me captive. Who am I without it? Though it may take a lifetime to answer, the moment I posed the question, I felt joyful, exhilarated—the way I imagine skydivers must feel freefalling through space. There is just life as it is: the wonder, the beauty, the pain, the mystery. Faith, even, that the ground will rise up to meet me.

For so many years, lacking confidence in myself, I searched for someone who could save me and make me feel whole: lovers, sages, gurus, psychics, therapists, healers. Finally, I got what I was after, but in the most surprising way. In a sort of cosmic joke, I went to Germany to be saved by the Divine Mother only to discover that there's nothing to be saved from. Not even fear, which, I see now, comes and goes, as insubstantial as a bank of clouds scudding across the afternoon sky.

An Itinerary of Faith

Susana Franck

During the Christmas holidays of 2009, I developed a serious and resistant strain of pneumonia. As doctors and nurses gathered around my hospital bed with somber faces—the various antibiotics having no effect—I kept telling myself that I could not die because I had not been married in church. Rationally, this held no water, because no clergyman worth his salt would have refused to bury me based on a civil marriage ceremony, but I felt I had not paid my dues to God and did not deserve a Christian burial. I also felt that it would have been hypocrisy to ask my family to give me a religious ceremony. God had been very good to me, and I had not reciprocated. It did cross my mind that I was scared and wanted to be sure I had God on my side, and that I was being superstitious. Or was I refusing to die? In either case, the conviction ran deep.

God has always been present in my life, although not necessarily in a very orthodox fashion. When I was a child growing up on
an *estancia* in Argentina, I associated him with the evil spirits (*los
cucos*) with which our *criollo* maids threatened us when we mis-
behaved. They would point at a drainage hole that housed a family
of toads and say, "There he is!" when a toad peeped out, and I was
convinced that God's wrath would shortly be visited upon me.

As the years passed, the toads returned to being simple toads
and my perception of God moved on to glitzier spheres. When my
Roman Catholic cousins were being decked out in fancy first-com-
munion gear (we were a very ecumenical family), God was someone
who required genuflection and crossing oneself, but also fancy
dresses that I envied. God also required incense, although incense-
filled churches made me faint. I longed for my cousins' ceremonial
church and their regal God, and I regretted that my parents were
arid Low-Church Anglicans who scoffed at all this paraphernalia.
They reminded me that theirs was a God with whom one could
interact personally; we did not need intermediaries. We could talk
directly to God, but there were no frills, no crosses, and no Virgin
Marys in flowing blue robes.

My father, who was English, had an education well grounded in
the Church of England. He could recite by heart all the scriptures,
hymns, and prayers, but was irritated by clergymen and never set
foot in church. He was the product of a very classical, moderately
narrow-minded education, and never questioned Anglicanism. He
was violently against the Roman Catholic Church and muttered,
"Popery!" whenever he was obliged to attend one of their ceremonies.

My mother's position was less well defined. She was an obedient
wife who did not cross her husband, but she would have loved to have
gone to church and been part of a congregation. My father scoffed at
her, so she meekly accepted staying home on Sundays. (Sixty years
later, with my father dead, she was able to prepare her own church

funeral in great detail, which was a consolation to her.) Despite her absence in the church, she managed to inculcate in my sister and me a rather basic knowledge about the Old and New Testaments, and provided structure to our religious beliefs. Under her guidance, I became a fervent reader of the Old Testament and a very minor authority on the Acts of the Apostles. What was perhaps most important, Mother made us aware of God's presence by making us pray to him (and not to Jesus) every evening.

Being a Protestant in Catholic Argentina was not easy. My sister and I were different from our schoolmates, cousins, and most of the people around us. We were not allowed to attend Catholic catechism taught as part of our school's curriculum, and we were obliged to follow courses in ethics and morality with the other students who did not belong—the Jews and the Muslims. The teaching seemed to consist of dispensing definitions of good and evil, right and wrong, and heaven and hell in terms of avarice, greed, and dishonesty. We were required to take copious notes and then illustrate the texts using fat boys to represent greed, piles of gold coins for avarice, blue sky for heaven, and red devils with forked tails for hell. Although I felt rejected by the system, I learned a lot about other religions and their practices. I also developed a tolerance that remains with me today, even if I abhor all forms of fanaticism.

By the time I was seventeen, I had been confirmed as Church of England and was technically a member of the Church. I had developed a rather personal and idiosyncratic approach to religion but was firmly convinced about the existence of God. I could cite many reasons why God did not exist but was certain there was some sort of a God—and that he was right there taking care of me!

At the time, and against the approval of my parents, I had applied for and won a scholarship to study in the United States and attend college in Pennsylvania. I had no money, no help from my parents, was alone in a foreign country, and from the perspective of

my very sheltered South American upbringing, was facing difficulties I had never imagined. Nevertheless, I sensed that I was backed
by an invisible, benevolent presence called God. I did not question
the fact that he had been singularly absent from the atrocious suffering of a great many people or that many others did not appear
to benefit from his far-reaching, generous support. He was neither
an old man with a beard nor a magnificent presence towering over
the world from heaven. For me, he was a presence that kept me
company, helped me, and prevented me from getting into too much
trouble. I did not pray to him and was honest enough not to ask any
favors of him. I just knew, in my self-centered way, that God was
there, supporting me.

During my student years and young adulthood, I rarely went to
church. Like my father, I was irritated by most of what clergymen
had to say, and I was not attracted by much of the sectarianism that
accompanied religion. Furthermore, I was into women's lib, political marches, the beginnings of a scientific career, and had little time
to devote to religion, which seemed like a homeland to which I
could return but was not yet ready. I was questioning everything
associated with established order and values. Nonetheless, I had
faith in God.

In 1969 I married Guillaume, a French, nonpracticing, assimi-
lated Jew. His family had not observed Judaism for three generations,
but they—along with their friends—were tied to it through intellectual
tradition and the sharing of common Jewish roots. During the Second
World War, he and his family had fled to the United States, where he
and his sisters, in order to simplify their integration and for security
reasons, were baptized Episcopalian. When they returned to France
after the war, they severed their relationship with Protestantism and
the connection with Judaism was not resumed. Anti-Semitism still
ran high, and being Jewish remained difficult. My mother-in-law was
a mean atheist and abhorred anything remotely religious.

For me, the family's religious no man's land was not a problem, since religion had been a sufficiently complicated subject throughout my formative years. Marriage in a civil registry office was fine. And why make things difficult by having a religious ceremony when we were unable to define the nature of the religion that should have been binding us! I was convinced that God would understand (even if, at times, I wondered whether some dreadful fate would not be visited on me).

But God and religion could not be easily shelved, and they came back to visit us when our two daughters (then ages nine and thirteen) wanted to be baptized as Catholics. With a hesitant Argentinean Protestant mother and a nonpracticing Jewish father, the girls felt the need to belong in our very structured and stratified French society. Most of our friends, as well as their friends and schoolmates, were Catholic, so it seemed natural for our daughters to become Catholic as well. Guillaume and I agreed that it was good for them to have a religious identity, and neither of us felt strongly enough to impose either Protestantism or Judaism on them. My father was no longer alive to be shocked, and my mother, simple soul, was happy that her granddaughters would not be heathens. However, some family and friends were shaken. How could we allow our daughters to embrace Catholicism? My father-in-law was pleased for the girls, and my judgmental mother-in-law expressed no opinion, which my husband and I interpreted as tacit approval. We were convinced that the girls had to believe in something, and I believed that God is not sectarian.

I soon learned that religion can be very sectarian! The process of getting our daughters baptized brought home that we were naive. Much like my childhood in Argentina, the priest in charge of baptizing the girls considered me an outsider. I might be a Christian, but I was not a worthy interlocutor, so all arrangements had to be conducted by one of my close Catholic friends. Deep down, I felt guilty about not having been a more assiduous churchgoer with a tradition to hand down to my children, but I did not allow myself the right to be offended. It was more important that my children belong to a religious community and benefit from God's protection as much as I had. (As it turned out, one daughter has remained an intermittent Catholic and has her children in a Catholic school; the other has adopted Protestantism, largely due to her husband, who is a rigorous French Protestant—as are most French Protestants, thanks to a long and savage persecution following the revocation of the Edict of Nantes in 1685, and the rift and exodus it provoked. French Protestants are a minority and have a characteristically strong group identity and solidarity.)

The next step in my daughters' religious journey gave me further food for thought: both of them wanted to be married in church. Their weddings, two years apart, reminded me (as if I needed reminding) that my wedding had received no religious blessing. Over the years, and from time to time, I had my regrets, but my marriage was a happy one. Yet again, I thought (perhaps somewhat complacently) that God would understand. Even so, I did feel a certain discomfort when faced with the pastor for one daughter and the priest for the other. Luckily, the pastor was open-minded, which made it possible for me to be frank with him. However, several years went by before we could delve into my feelings, and it was only when my health crisis arose that I was struck with a powerful need to be married in the church.

When I recovered from that near-death experience with pneumonia, I talked to my husband about my predicament. It was soon evident that while it was easy for me to envision a Protestant wedding, it was far more complicated for him. Guillaume is a kind, intelligent, and loving man, and he wanted to see things from my point of view, yet he did not want to betray his Jewish traditions and upbringing. The pastor who had married one of our daughters, and to whom I had already described our dilemma, is a learned and open-minded theologian who is well versed in Judaism. Perhaps he could help us to find a way to be married, without my husband having to violate any of his principles and traditions.

For almost a year, we met and exchanged thoughts and views with the pastor. He in no way tried to influence Guillaume but worked with him to clarify his position through intelligent and well-informed arguments. It was a difficult exercise for my husband, who had not shared my experiences. Whereas I saw this as a kind of preparation for my homecoming, my husband saw it as something of a revolution. In time, however, he came to think that the loving Protestant God was perhaps more to his liking than what he had been taught to view as the Jewish God of punishment and wrath. While he grappled with these views, my concerns were, in comparison, quite frivolous. What most bothered me was not how we defined God or faith but how we were to be married. The pastor thought—and in retrospect, I now agree—that our wedding should be a kind of official coming out in front of the church congregation. Whether it was because I am a very private person, or because I was daunted by the idea of a sanctioned commitment out of which I could not wriggle, I was downright terrified.

After much hard work, hesitation, and reluctance on my part, the pastor, my husband, and I agreed that we were ready to take the big step: a full-blown public ceremony during a Sunday church service. When we told our daughters, one was predictably and immediately moved and happy, while the other thought we were being ridiculous and would be the laughingstock of our friends and acquaintances. She came around, however, as she generally does, and was happy to host a little reception for us.

•————•

In 2011, Guillaume and I were married in a Reformed Protestant (Calvinist) church. We invited six of our closest friends, our children, our grandchildren, and my sister-in-law. A young bride could not have been more nervous. Between each of us having to stand before the congregation and read a text explaining why we had decided on a religious wedding ceremony, and then the actual step itself, my teeth were chattering. But once the service began, I saw my daughters and our friends mopping their eyes, and members of the congregation smiling, and I suddenly had wings. This was one of the most important moments in my life—in *our* lives—and here were those we most loved with a few we had never met, all participating in our adventure. God had been good to us, and now we stood before him, not only plighting our troth but answering his call. (As the pastor told us in one of our most convincing sessions—perhaps the one that played the most important role in my husband's acceptance of a Protestant wedding—"God beckons us and we respond.")

Our wedding was a commencement, as indeed all weddings are, but not the pots-and-pans-and-babies kind. We were embarking on a new and far more emotionally peaceful chapter of our life together. We found ourselves facing the challenges with greater confidence, better prepared to face the trials that were to confront us two years later, when I had to undergo major surgery. It was not that we envisaged the operation and recuperation with pleasure, nor did we have any illusions about the risks, but I entered the hospital believing that my affairs were in order and that I could face whatever had to be faced with serenity. Forty years of working in the field of cognition science had given me the tools to analyze my mental and emotional trajectory, and I was able to accept my intuitions about God—my faith—as a reality.

•———•

As someone who has devoted her career to the study of the brain and its functioning, I cannot avoid questions about the relationship between the mind and belief in God. A 2011 Harvard study found that cognitive style is an important indicator of religious belief, and this held true even when accounting for factors such as intelligence, education, income, and political orientation.[1] The more intuitive people reported an increase in religious faith over the course of their lives—a rise independent of religious upbringing. What does this mean? It suggests that belief in God is related to one's decision-making style, and those who rely more heavily on intuition have higher rates of belief. At the same time, those who are more reflective tilt toward atheism. By linking religious belief to intuition, the study supports the idea that there is something in the cognitive makeup of humans that promotes belief in a higher power.

When I was a student in the 1960s, intuition and emotion were not thought to be the object of serious scientific study: we had no proof of their existence. Since the mid-1990s, however, the neurobiological substrates of human emotion have attracted increasing interest within the neurosciences, motivated largely by advances in functional neuroimaging techniques. So how does emotion interact with and influence other areas of cognition? Research on intuition is forcing us to understand how human beings must have intuition (and emotion) and rationality in order to function properly.[2]

Popular culture and the dictionary are wrong to contrast intuition and rationality. Rather than being opposed to each other, they are interdependent. As G. Vogel reported in a much-cited article, which appeared in 1997, intuition would appear to be a bridge between subconsciously processed information and conscious thought.[3] Intuition triggers rational thought, whereas rationality, when well used, acts as a kind of filter to separate good from bad intuitions. I had an aunt who maintained that she possessed the mystical faculty that allowed some members of our family, including me, to determine the future. She insisted that I had "the fluid" and should put my extra sensory powers to good use. I found this unnerving and saw her as manipulative, merely interpreting what she thought people wanted to hear.

Later, I realized that she was talking about intuition, which is not genetic. Experienced scientists have intuitions that allow them to pursue some hypotheses rather than others; brilliant intuitions have led to major discoveries. A good chess player knows what move to take without having to think about it, and a good mathematician is guided by intuition toward problem resolution.

Despite years of hesitation and questioning, I *know* that God exists. I have no scientific evidence for why I believe in God, but I also have no indication to the contrary. Renowned atheist A. Richard Dawkins, who made his reputation on debunking God, admitted in a discussion with the Archbishop of Canterbury that he was an agnostic and not an atheist, because he had no proof against the existence of God. I certainly have not given the topic as much thought as he, but my intuition—coupled with reasoning—has led me to the same conclusion. Even if I still have problems with formal religious practice of all sorts, my faith in God is intact.

While I cannot prove the existence or nonexistence of God, I do think that faith is unavoidable. Everyone must believe in *something*, even if it is only in oneself. What is important is to decide what evidence we think is pertinent, how we can interpret it, and in whom or what we choose to believe. Science can show us how natural law works, but it cannot provide us with moral guidance or values to govern our lives. I'm grateful that my parents introduced me to a religious practice that allowed me a free dialogue with God and the possibility to make my way as best I could, and discover, if only rather late in life, that faith was an integral part of my person.

Our Shared Humanity

Frank Dabba Smith

In the United Kingdom, where I live and work, the Jewish population is sharply declining—with the exception of the separatist, ultra-Orthodox sects. I join many Liberal Jews who are especially concerned with the survival of a form of Judaism that includes, at its heart, universalistic humanitarian faith values and reason, rather than the emphasis on tribalism and arcane ritual. Our communities can be places where we befriend each other pastorally when it comes to life's intractable struggles, as well as being open to creative discovery and intellectual exploration. Furthermore, our activities could be much more open to people of all manner of background or faith (or of no explicit faith), so that they, too, might find renewal through learning about and experiencing a sense of the mysterious and an enhanced reverence for all life.

Such an open outlook also offers an incisive perspective when it comes to reflecting on a hugely controversial subject that is central to the concerns and, indeed, a primary expression of the faith of many Jewish people today: the State of Israel. Does any other subject arouse such passion—as well as animosity—between Jews holding different approaches to exercising their faith?

Following the Holocaust and the 1948 establishment of Israel, Albert Einstein wrote that he wished this new country to be a refuge for Jews, a place where they could live free of anti-Semitism, but also in full cooperation—government and economic—with the Arabs inhabiting the land. I've long shared this vision, but I admit that these views seem depressingly quixotic today, especially when juxtaposed with the harshly violent realities in the Middle East. More than ever, life there is suffused with forms of rigid tribalism and chauvinistic nationalism.

While living in Israel, I worked as a freelance photographer. One assignment took me into Gaza during the First Intifada in early 1988. During this excursion, I had an experience that forever reshaped my views of those I was indoctrinated to regard as my enemies. Together with my client, an American agricultural specialist working with the NGO Catholic Relief Services, I witnessed violent incidents involving the throwing of stones and burning of tires in an area of squalor. Not far away, our jeep broke down, and my client went off looking for help. A short while later, a small group of young Palestinian men approached. Quite isolated and vulnerable, I feared for the worst: these men could harm me and no one would be the wiser. I soon realized that they only wanted to repair the jeep. After a few minutes of tinkering with the carburetor, the engine roared to life. I opened my wallet and offered money, which they politely refused. "*Salaam alaikum*," they said and then left. I was stunned by their unaffected kindness and generosity. Since that day, my faith has been informed not only by a profound respect for the ethical and peaceful ideals of Islam but by an openness to others, regardless of background.

One terrible legacy of the brand of political Zionism that succeeded in Israel has been never-ending violence. Extremists and terrorists on both sides have preached exclusivity and have effectively held their own respective populations hostage for the duration of the conflict; a sense of victimhood has been used by extremists to justify their cause and the means to achieve their aims. Tragically, pain often doesn't teach us moral values, such as the virtue of universal compassion.

Thinking about the extreme example of Nazi Germany—and one must do so, as the State of Israel was formed in the aftermath of the trauma of the Holocaust—where an attempt was made by the Nazi regime to purge the earth of perceived enemies, based on a sense of victimhood and impending annihilation. In the end, this unquenchable and hateful quest for strength and purity offered only death and destruction to adherents and victims alike. Fascism and genocide, with their rejection of human difference and compassion, are eternal human tendencies hardly confined to any particular historical age or group. And yes, sadly, there are Jewish fascists too.

With respect to the Holocaust, my faith impelled me to examine beyond the surface appearances and blanket judgments. I learned in the 1990s that the makers of my camera, the Leica, had helped persecute people throughout the time of the Nazi regime. My curiosity took me to Germany to meet with the descendants of Ernst Leitz II of Wetzlar, who owned the factory. His grandson Knut Kühn-Leitz received me warmly, and together we have been on a quest to learn more about the altruistic efforts of his family. I am currently writing up my research as a PhD dissertation and, in doing so, situating the behavior of Ernst Leitz within a historiographical context, including evidence-based academic studies of other companies operating in Nazi Germany. This has been a fascinating journey both intellectually

and in terms of my faith, as I have discovered that courageously helpful human relationships can ameliorate, in some instances, the cruel
effects of the most hateful and persecutory regimes.

So where does this leave me and others who adhere to and wish
to express, in an active way, faith values consisting of a reverence
for all life, inclusivity, coexistence, and the cherishing of differences
with respect to the situation today in Israel and the Middle East? If
values like these lie at the core of my faith, how might I proceed to
act, despite coming from a faith perspective that is sadly marginal in
today's Middle East? Fortunately, there are a number of small non-
governmental groups that operate in the region and do not fall prey
to narrow nationalism and the need to humiliate or dominate those
who may be different.

In an attempt to express my faith actively, I became involved
with Friends of the Earth Middle East (FoEME), a group that has
been engaged in this way, and is devoted to restoring two historically
fascinating and environmentally unique features of the region: the
Jordan River and the Dead Sea. Over the course of the last century
and a half, the flow of the Jordan River has been reduced by over 95
percent (due to water being diverted), as well as polluted, by all sides
in the conflict. One result is the ecological disaster facing the area of
the Dead Sea as its depth decreases at the rate of one meter per year.
Not only do these critical water issues affect the health and welfare of
Israelis, Palestinians, and Jordanians living in the area of the Jordan
Valley and the Dead Sea, but the migratory route of hundreds of millions of birds dependent on the northern section of the Great Rift
Valley is also damaged.

Since its inception in 1994, FoEME has brought together coop-
erating neighbors from Jordan, Israel, and Palestine to restore the
Jordan River, and to engage in education and advocacy. Due to
such efforts, international awareness of regional water issues has
grown considerably, along with a sense that the physical environ-

ment must not be held hostage to any failing political negotiations. I feel hope because of the progress that has been made in improving water quality and in growing cross-border trust, despite the power of rejectionists emanating from both sides. Some of those who are very involved have come to view themselves as *citizens of the geographical region* rather than citizens of a national entity.

Who are these people working together for peace? They are all adherents of the three Abrahamic faiths: Judaism, Christianity, Islam—men and women who celebrate their differences as well as their similarities. All of them look to their faith as a source for instilling awe and reverence for nature as well as for their fellow human beings, regardless of faith (or no faith) or national background. People of no explicit religious faith find common cause and friendship, because the best of what are routinely considered to be solely secular values—humanitarianism and reason—are also respected by their explicitly religious colleagues.

How does my involvement in these humanitarian goals define my faith, my concept of God? Coming from a standpoint of openness with respect to human beings, how can I possibly limit an incomprehensible God though description? For me, the word *God* is simply a label signifying human projections assigned to overwhelming mystery.

If life is indeed mysterious and precious, then shouldn't my relationships with other humans be guided by gratitude, respect, and humanitarianism? To some, this may sound rather obvious, but given the prevalence of sloppy tabloid reasoning and sheer cruelty in our world, it is a constant, critical struggle demanding one's vigilant attentiveness and best energy. This ethically demanding faith neither accepts surface appearances nor does it accept that conventional might or popularity makes right.

As an artist-photographer, I've created a series of images that depicts the activities of EcoPeace personnel in the Jordan Valley.

Whether the subject is local Arabs teaching young Jewish volun-teers how to use ten-thousand-year-old technology to produce mud bricks at midnight, after the day's Ramadan fast, or the daily lives of people struggling to obtain sufficient water resources, we share the same dream: peace and justice for all. My faith that this will happen is greater than my fear that it will not.

My dedication to some sort of reconciliation in the Middle East now includes the participation of my wife and children. Together we support what we consider a cause that goes beyond struggles in that region. In our visits to the Middle East, we have been accompanied by committed Muslims and Christians who live near us in London. Our work in support of this organization offers friendship and greater community cohesion, and is a reminder to our children of the impor-tance of working together—of taking a stand, taking responsibility. How better to exemplify to them that the most appropriate response to the mystery of existence is to cultivate a shared sense of awe and reverence for the wonderful strangeness of life, here and now?

IV

·———·

This past year has changed my life. I never anticipated that during a winter's trip to Paris—when the air was so cold that parts of Europe were closed to train and air travel—a warmth would work its way into me and set me on a journey from which there would be no turning back.

Having lived in Paris for nearly five years, I was excited to spend time with old friends. Most of them were people I love, but I had always assumed they simply *liked* me. (Full disclosure: I share a birthday with Sally Field, so when she stood before the world, Oscar in hand, and announced, "You like me! You really like me!" she had my heartfelt support.) When I allowed myself to recognize—to let into my heart—the deep affection I was being shown, I was moved and surprised in equal measure. At first I wondered, *Why this change?* And then I had to look at the possibility that these friends had loved me all along, and I had been too anxious or timid to recognize it. If this were so, who else, what else had I been holding at arm's length? Other friends? My children? Opportunities? Faith?

The journey through life is so different for each of us. How many of us are afraid to look closely, honestly at all that we feel? How many of us recognize that we are constantly changing but are afraid to examine those changes? In my case, I've been taking the easy way out, ascribing my reluctance to aging and an overload of projects. What a perfect excuse to avoid scrutinizing my feelings! But in this past year, when I mustered the courage to take the risk of jumping in, rather than analyzing myself at a distance, I nearly drowned in the swampy mess of my beliefs. I resurfaced, looked around, and was truly, *wholly* afraid. I wasn't questioning only the meaning and importance of faith, of what I believed; I was also questioning the existence of God. In a way, I was taking a scalpel and drawing a line through myself, opening myself up with all parts exposed, digging through cells and tissue, sinew and bloodstream, in my search for my soul. It scared the hell out of me!

After I returned from my travels, I awakened often during the night, my head filled with questions about friendship and beliefs. I wondered why, during this particular trip to a city and friends I visit often, there was such a dramatic shift in me. Something was changing, I was changing, but what was that *something*, and why now?

Poof!

Aviva Layton

My husband, Leon Whiteson, died on August 25, 2013. The process of dying was neither serene nor peaceful—we had lived with a diagnosis of aggressive bladder cancer for over two years, and he'd been through the medical mill. Cystectomy, radiation, chemotherapy—"the full catastrophe," to quote Zorba. Finally refusing to go the experimental drug route, he chose at-home hospice. After a brief honeymoon period during which we both fantasized we'd be able to buy at least six good months, it quickly became apparent that Leon was down to his final days. His study, which had been filled with the paraphernalia of writing—a desk overflowing with Post-its, notebooks, lists, erasers, paperclips, Scotch tape—was now filled with the paraphernalia of death—a hospital bed, adult wipes, thermometers, medical gloves, an oxygen tank, pads, and enough meds to fill a pharmacy. He lay there for three days, drugged with morphine to block his intense pain, his body wasted, his face haggard, his only desire to die as soon as possible.

Friends and family gathered around to say their farewells and, although Leon was unresponsive, I was greatly comforted by their presence. There was one visit, however, I dreaded—that of our grandson, his wife, and their children: Hazel, four, and Silas, six. The children both adored their Grandpa (*Great-Grandpa* was too much to get their heads around), who used to play endless games with them, spray them with the garden hose, and help them gather oranges from our tree.

Although their parents were adamant about bringing the children, I didn't want them to participate in what was essentially a deathwatch. The thought that the last memory of their beloved Grandpa would be of him tethered to an oxygen tank, unable to respond, doped out on morphine, his mouth fixed in a grotesque rictus, was something I was absolutely set against, but their parents would not be dissuaded.

As it turned out, they were right and I was wrong. Far from being traumatized, both children understood that Leon was dying and stood quietly by his bedside. Later, Hazel asked her father to take her into Leon's room a second time. Staring at his closed eyes and unresponsive body, she said solemnly, "Grandpa was here and now he's gone. *Poof!*"

And that was as perfect an explanation as I'd ever heard of the enormity of what had happened in my life.

•———•

There's nothing more life-changing than death. Knowing that his death was imminent, Leon never once expressed the slightest interest in seeing a rabbi or a spiritual advisor, even though hospice kept suggesting one. After he died, I examined my thoughts for any trace of belief in an afterlife, a presiding deity, or even some sort of transmutation of energy, but I came up blank. For me, belief in a deity simply wasn't an option. If, as Jung posited, our concept of god is a collective fantasy, and every human contains a multitude of archetypes—one of which is god—then I must have been born one archetype short.

The only prayer I've ever offered up was when I was eight (I'm now in my eighties) and had lost my golliwog. Golliwogs have, thankfully, lost their popularity because they are possibly the most politically incorrect toys ever to be created. In the early thirties, however, the term *politically incorrect* hadn't been invented and so golliwogs were as ubiquitous as dolls or toy trucks. Modeled after a character in a nineteenth century children's book, these toys had coal-black faces, wild frizzy hair, protruding eyes rimmed in white, grinning red mouths, bow ties, red jackets, and striped trousers. They were grotesque, but I adored my golliwog and was so devastated I decided to send up a prayer to a god I'd always suspected never existed. I folded my hands, as I'd observed my Christian friends doing in school, and prayed silently. I can recall the exact words as if it were yesterday: *Please god, I don't really believe in you, but if by chance you're really there, help me find my golliwog.*

God failed me miserably. I never did find my beloved golliwog—which, to a deist, might in itself be proof of a god who disapproved of racism.

Although that incident wrapped up my religious ditherings, the invisible golliwog and the invisible god somehow became entangled in my imagination, and from then on, whenever someone mentioned god, I pictured him as a giant black figure dressed in striped trousers and a wide bow tie, grinning down menacingly on his subjects with a huge red slash of a mouth. A Golligod. (I was taken by surprise when I researched the word *golliwog* and found that, apart from proba- bly being the derivation of the term *wog*, it actually has a linguistic

connection to god—*golly* being an expression used to avoid taking
the name of god in vain, much like *crikey* is used to avoid saying the
word *Christ*.)

If I were brought up in any faith at all, it was the Communist
faith. I spent the first decade of my life calling Lenin "Uncle Ilya,"
and because my family and most of their friends were Russian Jews,
I assumed that all Russians were Jews who spoke Yiddish. Every
Sunday my father would take me to the Domain, Sydney's equiva-
lent of Speakers' Corner in London's Hyde Park, hand me a stack
of *Tribunes*, the local Communist paper, and send me out into the
crowds, where I would solicit sales by calling out in my shrillest
voice, "Support the workers! Buy a *Trib*!"

But there was another powerful force trying to pull me in the
other direction—that of my maternal grandfather, who was an
Orthodox Jew.

In deference to my grandfather's wishes, my parents would
allow me to accompany him to synagogue every Yom Kippur and
watch as the prayer-shawled men swayed with religious fervor, beating their breasts while muttering in some strange language as they
bobbed up and down in front of the *bima*. Somehow the idea that an
entity—*any* entity—would bother to take an interest in the antics of
old men with stale breath seemed neither probable nor possible. And
anyway, I reasoned, even if there were a god, why would he demand
to be worshipped and obeyed? To me, it was tantamount to my parents expecting me to worship and obey them simply because they
had created me. Surely the act of creation didn't demand eternal
obedience, let alone eternal love. As a recalcitrant and rebellious
child, that notion didn't appeal to me in the slightest.

Shortly after Leon died, I googled the streetscape of our house
in Los Angeles, hoping—in a moment of magical thinking—that
I might see him pottering around in our front garden. The way I
was able to guide that small hand straight to the minuscule spot of

planet I inhabited reminded me of the way people had spoken of god when I was a child—as a sort of Google prototype who could see what was going on in every corner of the world, however remote. He was the Supreme Googler, who could hone in on a Lithuanian *shtetl* on the Sabbath to make sure that my mother, Sarah Sniderman, hadn't committed the unspeakable and unforgivable sin of carrying her handkerchief (it was considered work, which was forbidden on the day of rest) instead of pinning it to the bodice of her dress. He could also zoom in on the lonely earth mass of Australia, sitting in the middle of the Pacific Ocean, target Sydney, then swoop down on that tiny *shul* in Bondi Junction to make sure my grandfather was *shockeling* back and forth in obedience to his commands.

But why this all-powerful god should care about whether my mother was a good girl or whether my grandfather prayed fervently enough was utterly beyond me.

And as I googled the garden, was god now googling me, recognizing my pain and loneliness? The answer, of course, was no.

•————•

The one who came to my rescue was my son, who insisted I join him on the Caribbean island of Tobago for the Christmas after Leon died, knowing I was feeling vulnerable and dreading the pain of facing the holiday season alone.

As we drove to a waterfall from our small fishing village on Christmas Day, we heard singing and music coming from a crowded tent set up in a parking lot. A steel-drum band stomped out hypnotic rhythms, which made it impossible to stay still. The whole tent rocked with dancing and singing and shouts of "Hallelujah!" Old people fanned themselves with palm leaves, children jiggled and bounced on their parents' laps, men and women swayed and raised their arms in the air, looks of pure ecstasy on their sweating faces. There was no sense of alienation or loneliness—their shared beliefs forged them into a joyful tribe. As welcoming to me as they were, though, I knew I was an outsider. The comfort of salvation and eternal life was theirs, not mine.

But then the pastor got up to speak, and I remembered yet again why I couldn't partake of their certainties. He talked of the recent floods, which had swept over some of the neighboring islands, and how, because god loved Tobago so much, their island had been spared the devastation. *But*, I thought, *didn't god love their neighbors, those whose homes had been washed out and whose lives had been lost?*

This is something I can never fathom, however many times I see or hear it in the media. A tornado rips through a town, leaving piles of rubble in its wake, but through some freak of nature, one house is spared. Or a mine has caved in, killing some of the miners but sparing others. Invariably, one of the survivors or ministers says that god was looking after them, that they were saved because of his love and grace. But didn't god love the people who lived in the house next door that was demolished? Or the miners who were crushed? Or the child who died in a fire from which others escaped?

The illogic, the heartlessness, and the sheer narcissism of those comments have always disturbed me. And, of course, there's always the vexed question of why an all-loving and all-powerful god would allow the Holocaust and other tragedies to occur. Believers have turned themselves into knots trying to explain those monstrosities. The parents of a child killed in Sandy Hook, former missionaries, when asked how god let this horrific event happen, responded, "God didn't orchestrate this; it breaks God's heart. This is not what He would choose." A god with gender? A god who didn't have a choice? A god with internal organs? Yes, it could have been meant as metaphor, but I suspect that, in most cases, it's meant as literal truth. As Ian McEwan has one of his characters say, "Among all the yearning rationales for the godhead, the argument from design collapsed with *Homo sapiens*."[1]

•———————•

I've always been fascinated by stories of how people lose or gain or change their beliefs—probably because it's never happened to me. (The Communist phase of my life came to an abrupt end when I realized that Lenin was neither my uncle nor a Jew.) There's the case of Edith Stein, who was born to a devout Jewish German family, but who later became an atheist and a brilliant philosopher. One evening, at the age of twenty-nine, she idly picked up an autobiography of Saint Teresa of Avila, which a friend had left lying around, and read it in one sitting. It was a *coup de foudre* moment. She converted to Catholicism, entered a convent, and became a nun, taking the name of Teresa Benedicta of the Cross. (Not that this saved her from the Nazis. Because she was born a Jew, she died a Jew in Auschwitz.)

Ralph Thomas, a Canadian writer and filmmaker, was brought up in Brazil by Canadian missionary parents who were strict Calvinists. He lost his faith when he was sixteen, while doing nothing more dramatic than crossing a street in downtown Toronto after having attended a lecture on John Calvin at the Toronto Bible College. It occurred to him as he was dodging traffic that if, in fact, god existed, he didn't want anything to do with him because this god was a dangerous entity whom he should avoid at all costs—just as he should avoid a speeding bus if it were bearing down on him. It then occurred to him that this dangerous entity didn't exist at all, and that the belief that had infused his life up till that moment was completely invalid. In other words, when he started to cross the street, he was a strict believer; by the time he ended up on the other side, he was an atheist.

My first husband, the poet Irving Layton, told me how he lost his faith. Born into a deeply religious Jewish family in Montreal (his father studied Talmud all day long, leaving the mundane concerns of earning a living to his wife), Irving slipped out of synagogue one Sabbath morning and decided to test once and for all the notion that

the all-powerful and often-vengeful Jehovah was a myth. Like all
Orthodox Jews, he was forbidden to do any work on the Sabbath,
and that even extended to switching on the lights. With much trepidation, he switched on the kitchen light and stood trembling, waiting
to see if the wrath of god would strike him dead. Nothing happened,
and from that moment on, Irving became a nonbeliever.

A similar thing happened to Leon. Although his family was not
orthodox, his father insisted on his son attending synagogue and fast-
ing on Yom Kippur since he'd had his bar mitzvah the previous year
and was now, according to Jewish belief, a man. Bored with the service and wanting to play tennis instead, Leon snuck out of synagogue
and arrived home to find his father sitting at the kitchen table, scarfing
down a cheese omelet. He never set foot in a synagogue again.

I'm surprised when some people become affronted when I tell
them I'm an atheist. "How can you be so certain?" they ask. "Surely
you mean you're an agnostic."

"No," I reply, "I'm not an agnostic; I'm a devout atheist."

One friend who is an agnostic was particularly irritated. "It's
like having a locked suitcase in front of you that you're certain is
empty," he said. "But what if it's full of untold treasures? How can
you be so sure it's empty?"

"Trouble is," I replied, "I've never even seen that suitcase, let
alone its contents."

Nor have I ever understood the intermediary stage of agnosticism. If god revealed himself to me in a way I could verify or find
meaningful, I'd immediately become a full-blown believer. Same
with fairies or elves or angels or unicorns or pots of gold at the end
of rainbows. I don't hold the middle ground about whether they're
real or not. I simply don't believe they exist, but if they revealed
themselves to me, I'd turn on a dime.

•————•

Being an atheist doesn't exempt me, as some assume, from believing in mysteries. There are many things for which there are no rational explanations. Telepathy, for example, which I've experienced in a very powerful way. My first marriage was a turbulent one in which we decided to take a break from our relationship with regular frequency. One such summer, while Irving was traveling in the South of France and I stayed behind in our apartment in Montreal, I ingested some LSD (this being the sixties) and had a powerful vision. I hallucinated that I was on a stony beach, running into the water, but just as my feet touched the waves, I looked back and saw myself as a stone lying on the beach. It was an intensely disturbing sensation.

A few days later I received a letter from Irving, and when I opened it, a poem fell out. It had been written while he was lying on a stony beach in Nice and was called "Ballad of the Stones." In it, he'd duplicated my hallucination to an amazing extent. When he returned to Montreal, we correlated our times and realized that the time of my vision and the time of his writing the poem were identical. Neither of us had ever had any experience of telepathy till that point, and to my knowledge, it never happened again. But there was the poem, proof that strange and mysterious things do happen.

That was a mystery I experienced for myself, and although there is not as yet any scientific proof, I've no doubt there will be. Same goes for the mysteries of the universe. I don't need to believe in god in order to experience the awesomeness or sublimity of nature. That thumping cliché about looking up into the vastness of the heavens and feeling infinitely small and insignificant is something I've never experienced. In fact, I've felt the very opposite—a sense of power that, as humans, we've created the very concepts of beauty and sublimity, just as we've created god in our own image.

This is not to say I haven't been envious of people who wholeheartedly believe in divine intervention, in the existence of an all-loving god, in forgiveness, salvation, and eternal life. Religion, says Philip Larkin in his poem "Aubade," is a "vast, moth-eaten brocade / Created to pretend we never die."[2] But life's hard enough, and we need all the comfort we can get, no matter from what entity, be it Jehovah or Allah or Shiva or Gaia or some diffuse Higher Power. Whatever or whoever gets you through the night, even if it means praying to the Great Golliwog in the Sky.

And though I've always eschewed the rituals of religion, I felt the need to dispose of Leon's ashes in some ritualistic way. They're now buried under one of his favorite flowering plants in our back garden. When Hazel's brother, Silas, asked what I had done with Grandpa's ashes, I showed him the mound that marked the place. He stared intently at it for a minute and then asked if his Grandpa would grow again. "I wish he would," I replied, "but, sadly, he won't." Secretly, though, I imagined waking up one morning and finding a baby Leon under the leaves. Or maybe he'd be fully formed, with his trademark mustache.

Meanwhile, unlike deists, I have proof positive that there is no afterlife. My husband was a passionate—bordering on the obsessive—gardener. I remember when he was well, he'd once remarked that when he died, his garden would die with him. I understood that. What I didn't understand was that when he began to decline, the garden would decline with him. As his cancer metastasized, so did the spider webs, the rampant vines that were slowly strangling some of the small trees, the giant raccoons who left huge mounds of scat all over the back deck, which itself was suffering from dry rot and termite infestation. In the last stages of his life, when he was prescribed steroids, which gave him a deceptively rosy glow, friends would remark how healthy he looked. He'd tell me afterward that he felt like a termite-infested house that looked wonderful from the outside but would collapse if someone slammed the front door. Prescient words both for himself and his beloved garden. It was obvious that Leon's garden was fast spiraling out of control, but he wouldn't hear of anyone interfering, even though he could no longer do any gardening himself. The result was that, after he died, I needed to hire a crew to chop down the dead trees, the strangling vines, the mounds of moldy leaves and mulch. During the first few hours of this cleansing, I had a feeling that Leon might come roaring back to defend his territory, but he didn't—absolute proof that there's no afterlife because, if there were, he would have reappeared, if only as some cosmic force. (I'm only half joking.)

Just as I wish he had roared with fury at the desecration of his garden, I wish he would come back as a ghost. Even though I've never believed in ghosts, I've always been terrified of them. Not anymore. I'd love Leon's ghost to appear at the foot of my bed, or preferably in it.

•———•

Death, as Julian Barnes put it, is "just the universe doing its stuff,"[3] and it did its stuff to Leon at 4:58 on Sunday morning, 25 August 2013.

He was here. Now he's not.

He was somewhere. Now he's nowhere.

He was alive. Now he's dead.

He loved me. Now he doesn't.

We shared a personal language, a dictionary of intimacy. That language is now obsolete.

I know his face better than my own because I looked at it every single day for the thirty-seven years we were together. I'll never see that face again.

I'll never touch or kiss or feel his body.

He hasn't passed away, because that presupposes he's passed away to some other place.

Nor, like my golliwog, did I lose him—that presupposes there's a chance, however slim, of my being able to find him.

He just died.
Ceased to exist.
Disappeared.
Poof!
Just as Hazel said.

In Memory of Leon Whiteson

A fierce man, a gifted writer, a dear friend
whose essay would have appeared here.
1930–2013

Keep the Faith

Christine Kehl O'Hagan

Although in her later years my mother went nowhere without rosary beads wrapped around her wrist and a tarnished Miraculous Medal tucked in her change purse (that she was forever handing supermarket cashiers in lieu of a dime), she was a young woman who went to Mass only under duress and referred to the solemn annual Blessed Mother Processions as "the goddamn nuns walking in circles."

My father, a convert to Catholicism, went to Mass every Sunday, but instead of sitting in a pew with everyone else, he stood by the door, ready for the quick getaway, obsessively checking his watch and peeking through the door's stained-glass panel, like someone waiting for a broken-down train.

When the ancient, cadaverous head usher once stopped my mother and me in the doorway of the packed church, and irritably informed her that I did not belong at the adult Mass but at the earlier children's Mass (where I'd been traumatized the week before when the girl sitting next to me passed out, pitching forward and landing on the purple leatherette kneeler in a puddle of pink crinoline, looking like a headless heap of cotton candy, and the boy on my other side leaned over casually and threw up on my shoes), my mother irritably suggested (*sotto voce* and at the top of her lungs) that the head usher "take the children's Mass and shove it up his ass," an inadvertent rhyme that made the congregation snicker, and gave my mother even more of a reputation than she already had from upending the shuffleboard table onto my father's foot one Christmas Eve in the Liffey Tavern.

•————•

I was a fretful, nervous child, confused, always, as to the quality and quantity of sin. Was I a *mortal* sinner or a *venial* sinner, an occasional sinner or a repeat offender? I went to confession every week just to cover the bases.

On my First Communion Day, I broke the string on my new "pearl" rosary beads and somehow managed to inhale four or five beads before sneezing them all over the marble floor. Then there was the Saturday afternoon I was coming home from Mishkin's Drug Store with a bottle of Miss Clairol's Copper Penny hair dye (that my mother was too proud to buy for herself), and brought it with me into the confessional, where I dropped the bottle. It shattered, the priest ran out of the confessional screaming like his hair was on fire, skidded in the mess, grabbed for the holy-water font but missed, then fell to the floor.

Or so I was told.

By that time, I was three blocks away.

Which was nothing (I assured myself) compared to the blond woman whose breasts were falling out of her leopard-skin slip as she ran down the church's main aisle, right in the middle of the Offertory, in gold, sling-back high heels. "Never love a man," the blond woman cried, waving her arms over her head like a pizza maker. "They're not worth it!"

"*Hmpf*," whispered my mother, sitting next to me. "I could have told her *that*."

Then we watched Big Joe, the Liffey bartender, who (it was rumored) had two bullets floating around somewhere inside his thick neck (and ties to what my Irish grandmother called "the may-fia"), grab the blond woman around the waist and drag her, crying, screaming, kicking herself right out of her shoes, past the altar, out the side door.

The priest's leg, semihidden under his ankle-length cassock, was in a cast, and he was off-balance (due to a little mishap with some hair dye). The whole church could have caved in, but that priest was having such a difficult time maneuvering about the altar, he would never have noticed.

When it came to entertainment, the adult Mass had the children's Mass beat.

•————•

These were my first thoughts on faith. All of these vignettes are true, all of them happened, and yet, as I started writing, I felt my Irish kicking in: the art of the mickey, the cut of the joke, a bit of the craic that has served me so well in my life, keeping me safe as a turtle underneath that hard Celtic shell.

But as I get closer and closer to my sixty-fifth year, the official start of old age, that shell feels too tight and, like short skirts, tank tops, gold high-heel slippers, no longer suits me.

A year or so ago, when a routine test suddenly went south and I almost died, I found nothing funny about the priest who came to my ICU bedside.

There were times in my early life when I found myself filled with what I call awe but what my child self thought of as *God moments*, or what the Irish writer C. S. Lewis called "stabs of joy." The first time it happened was in school on a dark, December day, when our class of forty or fifty kids was pasting snowflakes to construction paper. The room was warm and bright, and our gloves were on the radiators—the classroom smelled of soapy children and wet wool. It was the first time I'd felt *at* home when I was *away* from home. I felt a rush of love for each and every one of the other kids—a stab of joy that almost overwhelmed me. I felt the blood rush to my face, so unsettled by this God moment that I struggled not to cry. I sank back in my seat, staring around at the others to see if they'd felt any love for *me*, but if they had, it didn't show. From their oblivious expressions, cutting and pasting was what they were engrossed in, with nary a thought about God.

When I was eight and my five-year-old sister was home with the chicken pox, my father brought my year-old baby brother and me to Rockaway Beach. My brother, who had been to the beach before (though never without my mother), was terrified of the waves crashing onto the shore. He cried and wiggled in my father's arms, working himself up into a full-fledged attack of hysteria, and my father didn't know what to do. He stared at me, a frantic look in his big dark eyes. Though I had never had such access to my brother, my father handed him to me. I hugged him close to my chest, covering his head with a towel. I can still feel the heft and soft weight of that baby, destined for a short, difficult life, snuggling himself into my neck. *Mother*, I thought, awed by the possibility that I one day might have a child of my own.

Taking the long way home from school one bright autumn day, kicking through the papery red and gold leaves on the sidewalk, I found myself absorbed in their color and the crunching sound they made underfoot. It was one of those fall days when the air—in memory, even years later—smelled, however improbably, of cinnamon and apples. It was in that moment that I noticed, for the first time that I can recall, the natural world and its capacity for beauty, and once again I struggled not to cry. I yearned to share these emotional feelings with someone, but I didn't think the other kids would know what I was talking about. They were in the park, on the swings, sitting on a bench, reading Nancy Drew, while I felt myself stuck in a yearning kind of childhood that chafed and burned—like the unlined, red-wool leggings my mother insisted I wear.

It struck me that I was alone in myself and frightened because of it.

It was on a Thanksgiving night, after company had left, that I brought these feelings to my mother. She was standing at the stove, still in her apron, still wearing earrings. My mother never sat down to eat. She was always on the run.

"I'm afraid of being myself," I said to her, the only words my child self could find to describe my dilemma.

"Well, who would you like to be?" asked my mother, whose great gift was to go with whatever somebody said to her, like *Seinfeld*'s Kramer. (She and I were in a department store once when a toddler raced by us. We could hear his father calling him but couldn't see him. My mother caught the baby, picked him up, and turned to hand him to his father, who had not hands but metal claws. I stepped back, but my mother never flinched.)

I didn't know who I wanted to be.

But I'd been thinking about it, and what I decided was that everybody was stuck inside themselves, and everybody probably had these moments, whether they put it into words or not. It didn't matter if I had the right words or any words at all. Whatever my worries, whatever my fears, I told myself that my mother would be there for me—no matter what. Even if she didn't understand, my mother always understood

I look back now, through all those layers of years, and remember how she held my face in her hands that night and so many others. Then she fixed me a turkey sandwich and put the kettle up for tea.

•————•

The church of my childhood is where I first encountered grandeur. (Of course, I was such a nearsighted child that, with the lights and the music, it could also have been Radio City Music Hall, but never mind that now.)

It was a big brick church with embossed-brass doors—a church that was light and airy, and also rich with color, especially during Lent, when the many statues were covered in cloth of purple velvet. The domed ceiling had white clouds painted on an intensely blue sky. On brilliant sunny days the light pouring through the stained-glass window bounced squares of what looked like liquid fire onto the tile floor. Snowy white, starched Battenburg lace covered the altar, next to where votive candles flickered in little, red, fluted cups. The pews were the color of honey and, despite layers of oil soap, sometimes smelled of new wood. The priests' outer vestments were made of rich silk brocade and differed in color according to the liturgical seasons. There were burgundy curtains instead of doors covering the two confessionals, heavy enough to keep the gravest of sins contained within. (Not heavy enough, alas, to staunch the flow of Miss Clairol's Copper Penny.)

The Grey Nuns of the Sacred Heart, a French order, were my teachers; they smelled of Ivory soap and lemons (unlike the priests, who handed out our report cards and smelled of Aqua Velva). They were the Brides of Christ and wore slim, white-gold wedding bands on pretty hands that appeared unused—except for the occasional drop of fountain-pen ink or a smudge of chalk—compared to my mother's ever-busy, always-moving, work-reddened hands. The nuns had a way of tucking their arms beneath the bibs of their toast-colored habits that made me wonder if they even *had* human arms, bellies, legs—an illusion that worked so well that when the nuns went to the ladies' room, the more daring of the girls followed and peeked underneath the stall, expecting to find, I suppose, hooves or even wheels, like the ones my mother put on our childhood beds, three children in one bedroom with uneven wood floors, so that if one of us so much as sneezed, there was a pileup by the window.

In the church of my childhood, there was such beauty: chanting at High Mass, the *Domini sum dignus* ("Lord, I am not worthy") accompanied by bells, the hushed silence at the Consecration of the Host, the symbolic turning of bread and wine into the Body and Blood of Jesus Christ.

At the end of the Sunday Mass, new mothers were called forth for *churching*, a blessing for a married Catholic woman who had given birth in *legitimate wedlock*, a cleansing in honor of the Virgin Mary, who after the birth of Jesus and her re-entry into the world, was physically rather than symbolically submerged in water.

Mary, the Mother of Jesus: a woman revered in a church that has little use for women and is still run by men. A church where I once overheard an old Franciscan priest say, half in jest, to a woman with whom he'd been "playfully arguing," voice rising, face turning red: "I will not stand here and be corrected by a mere woman."

Mary, who offers her protection to Catholics, and in Catholic tradition, intercedes on their behalf to her Son.

Mary, addressed in my mother's *The Little Catholic Prayerbook for Children* (circa 1926):

> O Mary, mystic way by which Jesus came to us, we
> desire

> also to give to Him by thee; come then, O tender
>   Mother,
> come and take the children of thine adoption by the
>   hand,
> and lead them to the Blessed Fruit of thy most
>   chaste womb.[1]

Mary, the Mother of Sorrows, who stood at the foot of the Cross, and witnessed the terrible suffering of her beloved Son—words that mean more to me now than I ever would have guessed.

•———•

When my son Jamie died, I tried to lose my faith—just leave it somewhere like an umbrella, or a magazine I was tired of carrying.

I was angry with God for allowing Jamie, a kind, good, Irish Catholic *mensch*, to suffer, and oh, that boy, unable to walk, was the Fred Astaire of suffering, skipping its surface, never losing style or grace, and I was angry at God for then taking him away.

But I have another son, Patrick, whose wife, Nicole, has become our daughter and given us, in our grandchildren, Christian and Alanna, such joy, and I realized that anger and gratitude cannot sit on the same shelf, so gratitude is what I chose—how could I not?

Jamie was sick for a long time, but during that time (I realize now), we had help along the way. There was the doctor, a complete stranger, who was just about closing up shop one winter night when Jamie was sick and we couldn't get anyone else to look at him. There was Kenny, the respiratory therapist, who came every week and made him laugh.

I'm grateful for the laughter.

My husband, wearing a red-balloon hat, simultaneously pushing Jamie's wheelchair and dancing down the corridor of a catering hall after a Christmas party for handicapped kids.

There was the night that Jamie almost fell out of the wheelchair laughing at Patrick, who jumped up from the sofa, dropped his blue jeans, and mooned Yoko Ono, who was on television shrieking.

There was the time that the dog jumped into Jamie's lap, hit the control box, and turned the wheelchair, with Jamie in it, into a human-canine tornado.

Moments that, in looking back, were—*all* of them—stabs of joy.

Moments in the last year of Jamie's life when I felt God had intervened somehow, given us a last-minute reprieve, and moments when I knew that our luck wouldn't last.

There were times when I sensed someone—*something*—standing there beside us, as surely as you can sense someone reading a newspaper from over your shoulder, and that's why I'm a person of faith. It's that simple, that easy.

Tragedies happen, and I hear people ask, "Where was God?" and I think He comes to us in moments, and when we need Him, He's always there, standing in the wreck.

The F-Word

David Misch

I broke up with my girlfriend a while ago.
It was very painful—we had different religious beliefs:
she was an atheist and, at the time,
I thought I was God.

Many years ago, I was a standup comic who mostly did weird little conceptual bits. I only had one joke—the one above. It got good reactions, maybe because it takes a moment to decipher: "She's an atheist, he thinks he's God, so . . . Ah!" Figuring out a joke gives us a sense of triumph; we laugh partially at our cleverness in deciphering its mystery.

That bears a relationship to religious Faith. Religion takes life's greatest mysteries—Who are we? What do our lives mean? Where are my tennis socks?—and provides answers. When we take a leap of religious Faith, we're pleased that we've figured out life's answers, especially when compared to people who believe those other ridiculous religions (ridiculous because they're not ours).

The problem is religion doesn't actually help us solve any mysteries; it just asks us to accept someone else's explanation. It's as if you didn't like my atheist joke until I said, "Trust me, it's funny." (Trust me, it's funny.)

My area of expertise is comedy, so what the (you should excuse the expression) Hell am I doing in a book about Faith? Well, a form of faith is central to humor.

All jokes—and all comedy (and all narrative fiction, for that matter)—begin with a gimme: that a priest, a rabbi, and a gecko would go into a bar or, in a slightly different context, that a prince would hesitate before killing the king who killed his father. Accepting a premise is called *suspension of disbelief*, which is another way of saying *Faith*.

There's a contract between artist and audience. In comedy, accept the premise and you'll get a laugh. In religion, accept a higher power and you'll get eternal life, emotional support, and answers to all questions. (This may explain why there are more religious people than standups.)

• ——— •

"Knock, knock."
"Who's there?"
"God."
"God who?"
"Great, another atheist."

It's interesting that all surveys about the religious beliefs of comedians (note: there are no surveys about the religious beliefs of comedians) show a significant number of atheists and agnostics. My explanation of this (nonexistent) data is that skepticism is the Mother's Milk of comedians. A great man once said, "Comedy is life viewed from an angle." And I agree with me; it's almost impossible to view the world credulously, then make fun of it. Religions look at humankind and say, "This clay made of God can, by following our precepts, attain a form of divinity." Comedians look at humankind and say, "This clay, made of God, farts."

The reason farts are funny (admit it!) is that they're an implicit takedown of our pretensions to divinity. Yes, humans can dream—we have souls, we achieve achievements—but we also poop, puke, and pee. In other words, we're animals. (Do you object to being called an animal? Hugh Hefner points out the alternatives are minerals and vegetables.) And the sight of such gross creatures pretending to greatness is hilarious.

But not to religious people, for whom humanity's failings are tragic—proof that we need God's grace. For believers, Faith is a remedy; for atheists, it's a smoke screen which attempts to hide what it views as shameful—our human fallibility.

Let's look at some other points of contention between Believers and Uns. (I'm one of the Uns.)

Religion versus Mystery

Some believers say that taking away God leaves nothing; atheists say that taking away God leaves mystery. Humans love mystery, but only as far as there's a solution—a mystery that remains a mystery is irritating because humans hate disorder. Which brings us, logically, to the iPod Nano.

When the Nano first appeared, people thought the shuffle function didn't work because their favorite song would play or not play or play whenever they thought about it or whenever they *didn't* think about it. But the shuffle worked perfectly; the problem was people's interpreting coincidence as patterns. Paul Kocher, president of Cryptography Research, says, "Our brains aren't wired to understand randomness."[1]

I know a standup who plays a trick on his audiences. When things are going great and he's getting a steady stream of laughs,

he'll say: "My high school was so tough, the principal was Swedish." Or "My girlfriend's so fat, I don't know whether to take her to
dinner or a Dodgers game."

I await your laughter.

Nothing. But in the clubs, people laugh. Why? Because those
lines (which the comic calls "non-jokes") perfectly mimic the sound
of actual jokes, and the audience—liking the comic, and into the
rhythm of setup/punch line—assumes the non-jokes are funny,
ignoring the fact that they make no sense.

If people didn't reject randomness for meaning, that trick
wouldn't work. But if you're in a club and hear ". . . the principal
was Swedish," your brain searches for what that could mean until it
makes some desperate connection. (*Swedes are tough*?) It reminds
me of the intellectual gymnastics of bar/bat mitzvah kids trying to
interpret an impenetrable Torah passage.

Humans find meaning using pattern recognition. One evolutionary reason (and I just lost the Fundamentalists) (as if there were
Fundamentalists still reading) we're here and gorillas are in the zoo
is that we're good at guessing; anticipating what was going to happen
got early humans food and kept us safe. What started as a survival
strategy became instinctual, which means that pattern recognition
isn't just a human ability, it's a human need.

Imagine (since I can't afford the illustration) you're looking at
M. C. Escher's physics-defying staircase, the steps winding around
on themselves; you stare and stare, trying to make it make sense.
There's a scientific name for that effort—*pareidolia*: the mind interpreting sights or sounds as more significant than they are.

So you buy that, right? You've been tricked by optical illusions
and heard a voice in the night that was really the wind in the trees—
makes perfect sense.

Gotcha! Accepting that humans make patterns and meaning out
of chaos and meaninglessness leads us right to that merciless Faith-

killer, Existentialism, a philosophy which says nothing has inherent meaning, that we make our own. (That may be a slight simplification. Actually, have you ever taken a philosophy course? No? Then that's exactly what Existentialism is.)

Avant-garde composer John Cage said, "We really do need a structure so we can see we're nowhere." No one likes being nowhere. So our ancestors didn't actually discover our place in the world, they imagined it. They *willed* meaning into existence by using observable reality (animals, crops, weather, stars) to anchor their invented Gods, myths, and creation stories.

Since then, science has given us answers to many (though not all) of these natural phenomena. But The Big Questions—Why are we here? Tennis socks?—can only be answered by us. (Or, the religious would say, by religion.)

What I find provocative is that it's the religious who demand (and get) those answers. While believers claim to exalt mystery, they in fact deny it, because their answer to everything is God.

Interpretation Is Evil

While many believers believe they're different from unbelievers (full disclosure: I get three dollars extra for each use of the word *believe* or its variants) (shockingly, *Belieber* doesn't count), atheists believe they're the same: flawed human beings who try to work out The Big Questions using guidance from ancient texts, other people, and their own experience. The difference, atheists say, is with believers who claim that all answers come from the Bible.

Atheists' moral codes are adapted from the usual suspects— Plato, Aristotle, John Stuart Mill, and yes, the Bible—but they're up-front about that word *adapted*. Fundamentalists assert they don't "interpret" but simply follow the stated rules, although even the strictest Fundamentalists probably don't have ravens pluck out the eyes of children who mock them, as in Proverbs 30:17. (Personally, I've found it difficult to train ravens in the fine art of adolescent eye plucking.)

Take a simple, straightforward commandment: "Thou shalt not kill." Who could argue with that? And, thank God, no "interpretation" is necessary. But what about capital punishment? Many Fundamentalists say that's different because the Bible means *innocent* life (which is the foundation of their opposition to abortion). But where in those four syllables is the word *innocent*? When you assume that's what's meant, you're interpreting.

Fundamentalists deny that morality requires interpretation; atheists embrace analysis but also think believers, even (maybe especially) Fundamentalists, interpret just as much as we do.

Faith versus Morality

This question is often posed to atheists: How can you have morality without faith? But most atheists respond: How can you have true morality *with* faith? Atheists believe morality requires *choosing* how to act. Where's the choice if you cut and paste answers from a book? Have you thought about whether the answer makes sense, or do you just parrot someone else's words?

Atheists see ethics as principles that must remain flexible in response to the complexities of real-world experience. Frequently, people of faith twist the Bible's often poetic and metaphorical words to fit their own prejudices, ignoring the words that seem irrelevant, incomprehensible, or just wrong. (See *ravens* above.)

One could say (in fact, here I am saying it) that having to think through ethical issues is a more active, dynamic morality than unquestioningly applying preordained precepts. Atheists *work* to construct a moral life.

The faith based community thinks a world without religion would have no principles—that it would exist in moral chaos, with constant arguments over Right and Wrong, and endless conflicts between groups that disagree about what constitutes ethical behavior. Yet the overwhelming majority of the earth's population is religious, and that's what we have: chaos and conflict. The world's faiths not only disagree on many of the major (and minor) moral precepts, but there are battles, sometimes violent, *within* the faiths as well. (George Carlin pointed out, "God is one of the leading causes of death.")

Ask ten Catholics if contraception is wrong; ten Jews if eating shellfish is wrong; ten Muslims if music is wrong. How much agreement would there be?

Cold Comfort

Believers often point to giving comfort in times of loss or distress as one of religion's great benefits. Atheists believe that comfort is illusion, and choose to face disappointments and challenges using only our own resources. Yet how different is that from "God helps those who help themselves"?

Religion's comfort can be a cover for prejudice. People discomfited by certain sexual practices (I'm looking at you, Utah) (and the South) (and Africa) (and here endeth the parenthetical expressions) get comfort from believing those practices are condemned by the Bible, which justifies the persecution of gays as God's will. In fact, that's how some evangelists "explained" AIDS.

Still, comfort is comfy; does it matter if it's an illusion? I have a friend who, when sick, marches into her doctor's office and says, "Give me your finest placebo!"

One of America's most famous atheists accepted the need for comfort. Mark Twain felt that life is too hard and too sordid and too cruel . . . "without some mitigating influence."[2] For him, that was humor. (As a comedy writer, I urge humanity to reject its false idols and embrace sitcoms, political satire, and fart jokes. This would make the world a happier place and, as an added benefit, increase my income.)

But not everyone thinks comedy is the right kind of comfort. Mel Brooks famously said, "Tragedy is when I prick my finger; comedy is when you fall into an open manhole and die." That puts comedy on the wrong side of, say, Jesus, who was not known for mocking manhole deaths.

Plato and Aristotle believed all laughter was malicious, galvanized by the suffering of others. You need go no further than your local Loews Infiniplex to see audiences howling at humiliation. If laughter reflects cruelty, then surely any comfort it provides is, in contrast to religion, cold.

But what are we actually laughing at when we laugh at misfortune? In the movie *Bridesmaids*, a woman gets diarrhea, finds the bathroom toilet occupied, and drops her bare butt in the sink. Which gets big laughs. Surely it's cruel to laugh at the spectacle of a woman in horrible pain doing something gross.

Except . . . it *isn't* a woman in pain; it's the actress Melissa McCarthy pretending to be someone who doesn't exist, but who we recognize and relate to—a placeholder for *us*.

When we laugh at McCarthy, we're imagining ourselves in that situation—in which case Plato and Aristotle were wrong, because laughing at ourselves isn't cruelty, it's empathy. With a side dish of ironic amusement at how the noblest of God's creatures, the one endowed with the most intelligence, physical dexterity, psychological complexity, and emotional sensitivity, can end up squatting in a sink.

Critics of gross-out humor forget that while its gags exploit the gag reflex, what it really requires is empathy and imagination. Indeed, the depiction of pain is a timeless and universal component of art, from comedies with fat guys falling down to paintings of the crucified Christ. Being fascinated by suffering doesn't mean you're inhuman; it means you're human.

The text of that *Bridesmaids* scene may be pain and humiliation, but the subtext is the resilience of the human body and, by implication, the human heart. Comedy reminds us that life is pain, but pain is surmountable. Which is warm comfort indeed.

Comedy's not only Good, but maybe it's God. Sam Harris, a bestselling author on atheism, writes: "Love entails the loss, to some degree, of our self-absorption." I think the same is true of comedy. While we're laughing, we transcend our pain and failings in a timeless moment of ecstasy. Which is also how some people describe "seeing God."

•———•

> *It's funny how when politicians ask God if they*
> *should run for office,*
> *He always tells them to do what they intended to do*
> *in the first place.*

Maybe it's just point of view. Atheists believe that when a believer says, "I prayed and God told me to do X," it's the same as an atheist saying, "I thought hard about it and decided the right thing to do was X." How do you know when you pray that you're not just talking to yourself?

Faith. Belief.

That's not good enough for atheists, who say there's no proof God exists. And don't give me that "Every sunset . . ." crap; it could be Satan, or the Wizard of Oz, or the earth's orbit behind that sunset. (Hint: #3.)

Believers say there's no proof there's *no* God, but author Arthur C. Clarke noted there's no proof there's no Zeus.

In "blind faith" the word *blind* is superfluous; *Faith* means accepting without proof. But Science demands proof, in the form of reproducible results. We don't take the law of gravity on Faith.

If an atheist admits there could be some enigmatic, transcendent force that runs through everything, believers pounce: "That's God!" Whatever; semantics, man. But I can believe in that force without putting my Faith in it.

If the Bible's right that humans are made in God's image, it means that people are powerful and can use that power to give their lives morality and meaning. Graham Chapman of Monty Python said, "A murderer is only an extroverted suicide." Maybe atheists are just introverted believers.

I believe that life is mysterious and complex and difficult, and I'll do my best to get through it honorably, with faith in my friends and loved ones and heart and mind to guide me. Because, ultimately, I believe that to lose your Faith is to have Faith in yourself.

Grateful acknowledgement is made to Applause Theatre & Cinema Books (a division of Hal Leonard, Inc.), publisher of *Funny: The Book—Everything You Always Wanted to Know About Comedy* by David Misch (2012), some ideas of which inspired sections of this essay.

V

·———·

We often think (or are told) that personal struggles of faith are between good and evil. In my case, however, I see it more as the struggle between good and not so good. (And I admit that *struggle* has been difficult for me to define.) On one hand—the good hand—I desire clarity of vision. That is, the ability to recognize where my life is now and perhaps have the aptitude, the capacity, to determine where it is going. On the other hand—which I prefer to see as *not-so-good*, as opposed to evil—there is my lifelong unwillingness (read: horror) to feel emotionally or spiritually exposed. A private woman by nature (and I'm guessing I have significant company in this inclination), I will do almost anything to mask my emotions—especially where feeling overwhelmed is concerned.

Having admitted this, I must add that standing above the powerful coastline of Big Sur, waves booming against enormous rock formations and fanning sprays of water through the air, I am filled with a joy so intense that I sometimes cannot help but weep. And what is it that makes me pull off a highway at the break of dawn to stare at the changing sunrise, awed not only by its astonishing beauty but by the realization that this sky—these colors and formations—will exist for one brief moment, never to be seen again?

Jennifer Pierce, another gifted writer from my UCLA course, addressed the spiritual pull of Nature so beautifully:

> In the early spring of my fiftieth year, I had an epiphany while driving. On a hillside near Lake Saint George (in Maine) I saw the sunrise in my rearview mirror— a glowing red disc in a mauve sea of sky. Directly opposite, crowding my windshield, the full moon was setting. In this moment of almost perfect alignment, I was devastated by a familiar sense of utter aloneness, of having no one near to share that moment. I pulled to the side of the road. It was then that I knew I was truly glad to be alive—that I was one with the universe and, therefore, not alone at all. I also understood that my reason for being was simply to be a witness of such ordinary yet magical events in the natural world, that possessing human eyes connected to a human brain was an extraordinary gift of Nature not to be squandered. The miracle is in my being at all—that mind, body, and soul brought to light by the infinite looping of the universe at this particular moment in time and space, never to be precisely replicated.

Whether in heartfelt revelations or humorous riposte, moments of awe illuminate why and how we are sometimes moved to tears by the beauty around us—or why some of us turn around and walk away.

Drama, Mystery, and the Episcopal Church

Barbara Abercrombie

Six months before my second wedding, in my midfifties and happier than I've ever been in my life, I discover a lump in my breast—or rather R, my fiancé, discovers it, and I, not believing for an instant that it's cancer, make a joke about it, but the next day I go right in to the doctor for a mammogram.

This little pea-sized lump next to my left nipple turns out to be serious enough to warrant further investigation. So, along with wedding plans, I now have doctor appointments and then a biopsy scheduled for the same day we are to meet with the Episcopal priest who's going to marry us.

On a warm, sunny February morning in Palos Verdes, California, the three of us discuss details of the service—our vows, lighting the chapel with candles, the music, the white flowers on the altar. We

147

reserve the chapel for the evening of August 15, which is six months and three days away. I don't mention to the priest that we're going on to the hospital after this meeting, that I'm going to have a biopsy done on a lump in my breast. It's not quite real, more like a very peculiar dream I'm having. *Surgery in two hours.* Even our wedding seems like an event I'm dreaming about.

Before driving to the hospital, we visit the chapel. I've come here for the eight o'clock Communion service off and on for two decades, and last year we had a small memorial service here for my mother. I slip into a pew. I don't think of myself as religious, but I love the Episcopal Church and I love this small stone chapel. I believe there is something here, something beyond the material world—a spiritual mystery I can't figure out.

I have this strange sense of fate: if I have cancer, I have it, and praying not to have it seems a little late. Is this a lack of faith or simply being realistic? I lost the comfort of an easy faith years ago, when my beloved mother-in-law, at the same age I am now, died of throat cancer. We were smoking buddies who stayed up late at night, drinks and cigarettes in hand. She was my confidant, the one person I could call to discuss problems in my first marriage. She was always on my side. When she died, I stopped smoking. I also stopped believing in a God who could fix things.

Now in the pew, on my knees, I pray for the only thing I have any control over, the only thing that seems reasonable: courage.

•———•

For many years, I had a cozy faith supported by the beautiful rituals and music of the Episcopal Church that I had joined at age thirteen. Ritual, music, and taking Communion on my knees at the altar were important to me. My parents were Presbyterians (my mother, reared a Christian Scientist, and my father, a Lutheran, had decided that becoming Presbyterians was a good compromise), but they were dumbfounded by my determination to be confirmed in the Episcopal Church—and a little worried. Who knew? Next, I might become a Catholic.

At the risk of sounding incredibly shallow (but I was thirteen, after all), a large part of the reason I became an Episcopalian had to do with the tiny cups of Welch's Grape Juice and little pieces of Wonder Bread passed around on a tray by the Communion ushers in the Presbyterian Church. It reminded me of a party with bad refreshments, certainly not a religious experience. When I first attended Communion in the Episcopal Church with a school friend, I was deeply moved by the experience of leaving the pew, going up to the altar, kneeling, and being offered a little white wafer and wine. At thirteen, I wanted to be deeply moved by all things—boys, movies, books, and now . . . church. I loved to pray on my knees and breathe in the ancient smells of the church: incense, the dry pages of the hymnal and prayer book, candle wax, old wood. I loved *The Book of Common Prayer* and kept it on my bedside table—the 1928 version, with its beautiful, antiquated language. I believed in it all: God, Jesus, baptizing babies, and going to heaven. And I believed that if you stayed on your knees long enough and prayed hard enough, good things would happen and bad things would not. I had faith.

•———•

This is my first memory of discussing God: I'm three or four years old and my mother is scrubbing the floor. I remember the smell of ammonia.

"Where is God?" I ask.

"Everywhere," she says, without hesitation. When I ask her what exactly is God, she says, "Love."

The next thing I remember about religion is going to Presbyterian Sunday school and my parents giving me a Bible that had a zipper around its cover. I both loved this Bible and was embarrassed

by it. The only kid in Sunday school who had a zippered Bible.
I still have it.

•————•

I had never lost anyone close to me until my mother-in-law died of
cancer. When she went into the hospital near the end, I flew from
Los Angeles to Arlington, Virginia, to be with her. By then the cancer was so aggressive I could see it—tumors blooming like deadly
flowers rising up under her skin. Her daughter (my sister-in-law) and
I entered into that strange, dark world of the end, not really believing she would *die* but realizing things could not continue like this,
and therefore spending every waking hour with her. Finally, I called
her son, my first husband, and told him he should come. I prayed.
I wrote poems. And then one morning she died; she was gone.

I wrote more poems. I found solace in shaping her loss into
words, into the discipline of a poem, with images, details, and form.
Far more peace and meaning in poems than I could find on my knees
in a church.

I had never really thought deeply about religion; I had always
felt it instead. As if I were wandering through a spiritual cafeteria, I picked and chose. I believed I could have options, selecting
only those things that made me happy. Music, incense, Communion
at the altar, prayer on my knees, the 1928 version of *The Book of
Common Prayer*—these were my choices. But now I found myself
facing a cold wall of disbelief. Jesus, Son of God? God? How do
you fit a belief of God into seeing someone you love die of cancer?

But I still wanted and needed a spiritual practice. Maybe I'd
become a Quaker or a Buddhist. Then I wouldn't have to deal with
the Bible or Jesus. Zen Buddhism appealed to me . . . the pottery, the
tea service. I doubted I was a Christian anymore, let alone a believer
in God. Art seemed more spiritual, made more sense to me than
religion.

A few years later, I took a course on world religions taught by a former Catholic priest. The Bible is all metaphor, he said, giving me sudden permission to think of it and all of religion that way. Christianity suddenly made sense to me. Transformations and resurrections. Blood into wine, flesh into bread, walking on water, and all the rest of it. God was love. God was everywhere. Religion was essentially poetry, one huge metaphor.

That I could understand. A zippered Bible was also a metaphor.

• ———— •

It's Valentine's Day, and R and I are in his kitchen, waiting for the biopsy report. I've always thought of Valentine's Day as one of those hyped holidays meant to sell a lot of candy and flowers, like Mother's Day, that causes vast numbers of people who don't have a lover (or a mother or a child) to feel depressed and left out. Consumerism at its worst. I'm feeling cranky today. But in spite of my bad attitude, R has given me a present: a beautiful watch. I can hear it ticking on my wrist in the silence. If this were a poem or a scene in fiction, I'd write the ticking into a big deal, another metaphor.

Finally, the phone rings.

So sorry. But it's bad news, says the doctor. It's cancer—and he'd been so sure I didn't have cancer but it is cancer and he is so sorry. His voice goes on and on, and the kitchen tilts. R holds me. I feel like I'm in a very bad movie—the kind in which the minute someone gets told they have cancer, you know what's going to happen to them by the end of the movie.

In the middle of the night, when I can't sleep, I write in my journal. Nothing very articulate or profound, just fear and attempts at bravado. Finally, I wake up R and tell him I'm afraid I'm going to die. "You can't die," he says, "you're getting married next summer."

I have a lumpectomy and lymph-node dissection, and then six weeks of radiation is scheduled. Now we wait to hear the results of the lymph-node test. Has the cancer spread?

I've started reading books about breast cancer, self-healing and faith, the immune system. I'm pretty skeptical of most of it, but I do wonder if my immune system crashed and burned during the recent six-year period when I lost both my parents and went through a divorce. Weirdly, the tumor was right over my heart. On the other hand, if you get cancer because you go through loss and a bad time, wouldn't everyone over the age of thirty have cancer? Who on this planet doesn't go through losses and bad times?

But how does faith fit into all of this? If I believe that God will heal me, he will? That if I have a positive attitude, I won't die? But does this mean that if I do die, it's because I didn't believe or pray hard enough? That I'm a loser and had a crappy attitude? I don't believe any of this.

My friends—Jews, Episcopalians, Catholics, Mormons, Buddhists, born-agains, even atheists—say they are praying for me. Do I have faith that those prayers are being heard? The word *faith* suddenly begins to sound kind of fuzzy, a bit out of focus. Like prayers floating heavenward on little puffs of clouds. I do believe in the meditation aspect of prayer and the notion of positive energy from prayer somehow flowing out into the universe. I do believe in miracles too; I'm just not sure of the cause-and-effect angle.

We continue to wait for the results of the lymph-node dissection. Test results hold you hostage. I'm not thinking deep and spiritual thoughts at this point; I certainly don't pray. I don't bargain with God. There's just trivia in my head: I'll buy Tina Turner wigs and smoke pot if the cancer has spread and I need chemo.

Again, there's a phone call, and this time it's good news. The cancer hasn't spread, and I'm filled—*flooded*—with gratitude.

I go through radiation. I do not "battle" breast cancer, that cliché the media always uses. It's been caught early. I have insurance and good doctors; I'm incredibly lucky. And I'm not a *cancer survivor*, another term that annoys me to this day. I'm being treated for cancer, and I will get over it. My friends and family members who did not survive were not losers. Why would a God who let some of my friends and family die of this disease allow me to live? Allow me to call myself a survivor, as if I personally accomplished the feat of staying alive?

I've never asked, *Why me?* but instead, *Why not me?* I did not, as some preach, cause my own cancer by hiding emotions or not taking care of myself. There is so much psychobabble about breast cancer that it makes me crazy. And all those damn pink ribbons.

What do I believe? I know for sure that I believe in the power of words and art and music and drama to heal the soul. I believe in the transformation of art—that art can turn pain and hardship into meaning and light. I believe in living a spiritual life through the arts. I also believe in laughter, yoga, running, and I believe that animals and Nature offer comfort and solace, and are as close as I can get to God. I believe in loving my family and friends with all my heart, and being loved back. I believe it doesn't hurt to get down on your knees once in a while and pray.

•———•

On August 15, I walk down the aisle on my brother's arm, in the same chapel where I sent up prayers for courage six months before. I think that finding courage, moving from an unsafe place to a safe one, takes luck. Our five children, my two and his three, stand with R at the altar. The chapel is filled with candlelight and the faces of people I love. White flowers glow on the altar, the organ plays "Sheep May Safely Graze." My brother maintains I became an Episcopalian because of the drama—and he's right, of course. But why do I stay in the church and love it so fiercely, while at the same time there is so much in it that I don't believe, don't understand?

At the altar, R vows to love me; comfort me; honor and keep me in sickness and in health, forsaking all others, and to be faithful to me as long as we both shall live, until we are parted by death. Vowing to have and to hold from this day forward, till death do us part not only turned out to be inaccurate in my first marriage but sounded different when I was twenty-four. Death was so far off into the future that the whole idea of dying was shrouded in mists of time and improbability.

•———•

I keep wondering, *Why me? Why am I so lucky?* Is it the roll of the big dice in the sky? Genes? I can't say that I had *faith* that I'd survive. I had hoped for the best; I was lucky. But I do have faith in this new journey I'm on—my marriage to R, our new family. It's the spiritual mystery I continue to grapple with.

Maybe faith is being able to abide with the mystery while not knowing the answers. Maybe the answers can't come through your head but only through your heart. Maybe religion is, after all, to be felt, not analyzed. Maybe part of the mystery is how faith can renew itself over and over.

Portions of this essay have been adapted from the author's memoir, *Writing Out the Storm*, published by St. Martin's Press in 2002.

Razor-Edged Abyss

Carrie (Cariad) Kabak

Father Dougal: *God, Ted, I've heard about those cults.*
Everyone dressing in black and saying Our Lord's going to
come back and judge us all.
Father Ted: *No, no, Dougal, that's us. That's Catholicism you're*
talking about there.

—*Father Ted*, series 2, episode 4

The class has until last bell to create a collage entitled *Our Depiction of Hell*. One more hour to go—surely plenty of time to produce a piece worthy of a Holy Picture reward.

"More fire please," says Mrs. MacKeon. "More soot and ashes and smoke. Add a chunk of burning coal. Splash it all over with red and yellow sparks. Hell is a blistering, razor-edged abyss," she says. "A pit of searing heat and ceaseless clamor. Listen, listen," she says. "Listen to the story of Lady Fátima again and *concentrate* this time. Be inspired. Be creative. Reveal what lies in wait for any unfortunate who chooses to reject the Divine Father.

"In 1917 three shepherd children were tending their flock about two miles west of Fátima in a town near Ourém in Portugal. Suddenly, a flash of lightning revealed a dazzling apparition of the

155

Virgin Mary, radiant in white light, standing amongst the leaves of a small holm oak . . ."

Mrs. MacKeon's voice drones on in the background.

Waiting for the dramatic part of the tale—the bone-chilling, blood-curdling crescendo—a ponytailed girl studies the bumps on her fingers. Padded by cushions of skin, they started to grow when she joined Our Lady of Sorrows, a school where every lesson, be it English, algebra, religious studies, or even art, is grueling and arduous, challenging and grim. Where filling page after page of an exercise book with inked words and scrubbing sugar paper with wax crayons and drawing geometric shapes precisely with Cumberland pencils has made her right hand look just like Mamgu's.

At least the bumps don't hurt, no matter how hard the girl sinks a tooth into them. Whereas Mamgu, her poor grandmother, has to keep knitting striped pullovers to keep what too often amounts to *crippling* pain at bay.

Mamgu calls her granddaughter *Cariad*. Her loved one. She helped her knit a scarf using 100 percent–washable navy worsted. It matches the compulsory school blazer better than the turquoise the child's mother returned to Arden's Haberdashery.

Shame, really—Cariad loved that warmer shade of blue. It reminded her of Our Lady's sash. The peaches-and-cream yarn, which was her second favorite, brought angels' wings to mind. Mamgu has noticed, with sorrow in her Welsh heart, that her granddaughter's head is full of Catholic notions these days—and whatever else that school, Father Murphy, or her mother, Biddy, is constantly drumming into her brain. It's just not right.

"Our Lady showed the three children a great sea of fire," says Mrs. MacKeon.

Here it comes.

A spontaneous shiver zips through Cariad's body as she pays attention to every rise and fall of her teacher's voice.

"Our Lady showed the three children a great sea of fire, which seemed to be under the earth. Plunged in this fire were demons and souls in human form . . . all blackened or burnished bronze . . . now raised into the air by flames that issued from within themselves . . . now falling back on every side . . . without weight or equilibrium, and amid shrieks and groans of pain and despair . . ."

"Jesus Christ," says Cariad's friend Clara. "Who would dare reject the faith knowing *that* was in store?"

"The demons could be distinguished by their terrifying and repulsive likeness to frightful and unknown animals . . ."

"I will never miss Sunday Mass again," says Cariad.

Where one is fed with abundant graces and nourished by the Word of God.

When her parents were away in Ireland, Cariad was told to attend Mass by herself. That Mamgu, along with Griff, her grandfather, would be waiting with breakfast upon her return. But Cariad stayed in her attic bed instead, because the solitary walk along Chinnridge and Tixell is a long one that involves bike alleys and dual carriageways and roundabouts and too many zebra crossings. The prospect of negotiating the school route on a Sunday did not appeal to her. Soothed by the jingle and jangle of Mamgu and Griff washing and drying dishes below, she soon fell back asleep.

Unfortunately, Biddy won't allow her daughter to take a shortcut through the Dingles, a place that's riddled with streams and crisscrossed with dirt paths. It's strictly out of bounds. It's where Kitty Dooley lives, a girl in Cariad's class who eats hedgehogs for supper and who rides her very own Tinker Pony.

Cariad's grandparents had no intention of forcing the issue. A childhood in Carmarthenshire that revolved around Sunday school, sermons, and severe indoctrination was enough for them. But later, despite saying, "Such nonsense, *bach*!" they could do little to dismiss the child's belief that she had committed a mortal sin. The bacon and mushrooms Griff served on fried bread did nothing to raise her spirits. Nor did a bag of Pascall Jubes, her favorite sweets above all.

"My soul is tarnished," says Cariad. "For evermore."

"*Arrah*, shut up," says Clara. "Sure, everyone misses Mass once in a while. A quick round of the rosary and your soul will be whiter than snow."

Mrs. MacKeon suggests the two girls at the front should stop whispering and kindly get on with their work, please. The penalty will be Sellotape on the lips if she hears any more. A rap with the ruler if she's pushed too far.

Cariad has been taught that dedication to one's faith, plus constant obedience, is the only way to avoid earthly punishment—or far worse than that—eternal damnation. And so she sharpens her pencil while plucking up the courage to tackle Satan, that embodiment of evil, that destroyer of souls, that enemy of righteousness himself. She soon discovers he demands a black outline, or else he'd be lost in what Clara considers the best swirling torment she's ever seen.

"You're a pure genius," she tells Cariad.

Which is when Mrs. MacKeon gives them a final warning.

Meanwhile, a radiator with iron ribs cranks out way too much heat for a small classroom on an autumn day. The muggy atmosphere adds to the pressure of trying to add horns, cloven hooves, sheep's eyes, and other such devilish details to Satan before the last bell, and soon becomes overwhelming. It's an enormous task. A bleak and highly disturbing project. And so Cariad is relieved when Mrs. MacKeon grants everyone just one more lesson on Monday to finish it off.

The next collage, she reminds the class, is due by Christmas, and will feature *Our Understanding of Purgatory*. Finally, *Our Interpretation of Heaven* will bring the mission to an end, and in turn, celebrate the class's First Holy Communion.

On the way home, Cariad's school uniform soaks up the rain like blotting paper. Her ponytail turns into rats' tails. Her shoes squelch.

Her pleated skirt clings. Her kneesocks slide down to her ankles, sopping wet. As she leaves Chinnridge Road, she is drenched by a deluge of pitchforks, and as she approaches Lowbrooke, a car skims a puddle, leaving her spattered with drain muck and mire.

She raises her head to see if she has reached the horse-chestnut tree yet—the halfway mark on Tixell Road. Her dad is still at work—both parents are—so who could be meeting her? Standing there. In a plastic raincoat. Who *is* that man?

He is short in stature, and his umbrella is black and vast and wide. He asks if Cariad would like to take shelter until the storm passes. What about a hot cup of tea? It's all right, he says. His wife is at home. Come on.

He has a smiling, dimpled face. Two buttons for eyes.

"What's your name?"

She tells him.

She can see the horse-chestnut tree.

Only a stone's throw away. Heavy with rain and conkers.

And the latchkey is already in her hand.

The man is very kind, but no thank you.

And she soldiers on, thinking no more about it.

•————•

According to Biddy, their new carpet at 315 Kingswood Lane is a *festoon* of jewels. Not only is it infused with gold but also spangled with rubies, sapphires, and jade.

After changing her clothes, Cariad sits cross-legged on the thick pile. She secures a dishcloth on her head with a length of twine to imitate what the saints and disciples wore, as did the shepherds, when the angels descended from heaven. When glory shone around.

She allows herself to fall into a trance, and before long, patterns on the wallpaper begin to merge together. Through half-closed eyelids, she looks for shapes to fashion into a Jesus with a burning sacred heart. A Holy Spirit with wings. And a Virgin Mary with an entourage of cherubim, their hands all clasped in prayer.

Cariad calls this phenomenon the Mysterious Transformation.

There's usually plenty of time to play visions until her parents come home.

However, as she relives the story of Our Lady of Fátima, she is overcome by a sense of dread and decides to cut this particular session short. Such gruesome fantasies, such persuasive illusions—all are too real for her, making her ignorant and unmindful of the dangers that are closer to home.

• ———— •

Father Durkan, the visiting priest, has a voice like syrup. He's immaculate, spick and span, and the spitting image of Kookie from *77 Sunset Strip*. So no wonder half the girls in class are in love with him.

Following their very first confessions, Cariad and Clara compare notes. As for sins, they had both used a couple Mrs. MacKeon had suggested, which were added to a nifty little number of their own.

Father Durkan was undoubtedly impressed. They both saw him smiling through the grille, after all.

"Look, here comes Kitty Dooley," says Cariad.

"Well?" says Clara.

Kitty plonks her hands on her hips. "He did nothing but play with himself," she says. "He started at 'Bless me Father,' and was still at it when he gave Absolution."

"We don't believe you!" says Clara.

Cariad shakes her head. "You are nothing but disgusting, Kitty Dooley."

"Priests don't do things like that!" says Clara, wagging her finger. "They are *vessels of Christ*."

"On me mother's grave," says Kitty, stomping her foot. "I'm telling the truth!"

"*Arrah*, shut up," says Clara. "Liar, liar, pants on fire."

And with that, she takes Cariad's arm and they march off with ponytails swinging and fingers snapping, and them singing *77 Sunset Strip* . . .

"Hoi!" shouts Kitty Dooley. "His John Thomas looked like an ould earthworm. I saw it with me own two eyes!"

"Don't listen to her," says Clara. "She's full of gobshite."

Only a week later, Father Durkan's dismissal is shrouded in mystery. A secret to be concealed. An event barely discussed and soon disregarded.

And the reputation of both the school and the church was thus preserved.

•———•

The smell of incense, made of frankincense and myrrh, wafts through Our Lady of Sorrows RC Church. There's a swish of vestments as feet *tap-tap* over stone tiles. Checkered tiles, gray and beige, arranged like a chessboard. Father Murphy and the altar boys travel along ranks, files, and diagonals to reach their positions. Forward, backward, to the side, sedately, reverently, one square at a time. Parents, guests, and relations in their finest attire muffle coughs, adjust hats, and straighten ties in readiness for what promises to be a momentous occasion.

The combined *Our Depiction of Hell, Our Understanding of Purgatory*, and *Our Interpretation of Heaven* is displayed under the Stations of the Cross, stretching all the way from *Jesus is Condemned to Die* to *Jesus Falls the Second Time*. And now Mrs. MacKeon arrives, in her crimplene suit, to lead her class through the entrance hall, which is tastefully decorated with tapered candles and an arrangement of toad lilies.

The boys are drilled to the left.

The girls to the right.

Cariad's the one wearing the dress with the puffed sleeves and piecrust neckline. When the choir is halfway through *Panis Angelicus*, she's nudged forward by the touch of a fist, soft in her back. As she treads the tiles, her new Mary Janes squeak and her headpiece slips to one side, but she's nearly there now. And when she reaches the finishing line, she grabs hold of the altar rail as if she were on a sinking ship.

"Beautiful," whispers Mrs. MacKeon. "You're all doing fine."

"Me fecking knees are knocking," whispers Kitty Dooley. "I'm scared to death."

"Watch yer mouth," says Clara. "You're in the presence of God."

Cariad lifts her chin to meet the Savior's gaze. Every muscle of His body, every sinew, every vein, is so realistic, it's hard to imagine He's carved out of wood. Rivulets of sweat course down His neck. Blood drips from lifeless fingers. Thorns pierce, nails penetrate, and ropes bite into delicate flesh.

It's an amazing crucifix.

Cariad tries to absorb His quiet endurance, sense the ache in His heart, and experience the same pain. It's her First Holy Communion, and she waits for respect to explode into something new and far more wonderful. For once that happens, she shall be at peace and in a permanent state of adoration.

Still completely oblivious to the real world around her.

•———•

When the final term at Our Lady of Sorrows arrives, mothers in the parish discover the Communion dresses they held back are too small for the Sacrament of Confirmation. So there's a flurry of borrowing and buying or all-night stitching of satin and silk and taffeta and tulle. And the bishop anoints Cariad's class with the Holy Chrism, and the children are thus sealed by the Spirit before the cramming and coaching begins. For they must soon undergo a three-paper ordeal called the Eleven Plus, an exam that will govern their admission to a prestigious convent school—or to the secondary modern down the road.

After posing for snaps with members of the church hierarchy, the parents *et al* are ushered home while the children are treated to a feast of finger sandwiches. Canned salmon. Spam. Slices of processed cheese. And Shippam's meat or sardine paste on a layer of margarine.

Cariad savors her last spoon of jelly, which was full of pineapple-chunk surprises.

"We never eat this shite at home," says Clara, "But if truth be known, I'm finding it downright delicious."

"Me belly's groaning. I'm as stuffed as a goose," says Kitty Dooley. "Will ye come with me to Cleve Park?"

No one else will. It's only Cariad and Clara who allow her to double skip with them. "In, in, a bottle of gin, they sing. We call our friend Kitt—y in."

"It's grand at Cleve Park," says Kitty. "Great *craic* altogether. Me brothers love the monkey bars."

For Cariad, the tinker girl has become a fascination. How she lives. As free as a bird. How she smells like bonfires, and how she doesn't care that her lace-ups are really boy's shoes. Or that her cardigans are always rolled up at the sleeves, three sizes too big.

"How can we play in this getup?" Clara wants to know. "And isn't Cleve Park the other side of Scribner's Hill?"

"A mile away is all," says Kitty.

"I'll ruin my bolero," says Cariad.

The one Mamgu made, with rabbit-hair yarn.

"Sure, we'll only spend half an hour," says Kitty. "What harm?"

The sun is a-dazzle outside, sending flitters of light over the assembly floor. What better day to visit a playground? The girls shrug on their anoraks and stuff their veils in carrier bags that hold a myriad of Confirmation gifts. Missals, rosaries, keepsake boxes, and Holy Spirit lockets.

•————•

Cleve Park has a witch's hat that rocks and sways as it circles, and comes to a stop with a shuddering *clank*. It has a sheer drop of a slide with an iron ladder and a wire cage at the top. It has a round-about with peeling paint that spins as fast as Cariad, Clara, and Kitty Dooley can scoot, one leg on and one leg off. And swings with splin-tery seats that hang from chains, and a spider's web that reaches breakneck speed while spitting gobs of grease.

Pitch-black grease that leaves stains on their dress hems and cancan petticoats. "Our mams will kill us," says Clara. "We'd best head home and face the consequences."

Tom, Cariad's dad, is pulling into the driveway about now, after working time-and-a-half at the ICI (Imperial Chemical Industries). He's looking forward to putting on his slippers, lighting a cigarette, and watching *Dixon of Dock Green* on telly. And Biddy is about to step off the No.11 bus at the terminal, having spent the five-pound budget on the usual round of beef, leg of lamb, and list of groceries.

•————•

In the Dingles, Cariad and Kitty Dooley tramp through ferns, rushes, and hogweed, following the course of Sarehole Brook. They brush past knapweed, ragwort, and musk mallow, and tread over carpets of wild garlic, pungent in the wet flushes and ditches. When they reach a clearing, between the hawthorn and beech, "See those elderflowers?" says Kitty. "Me gran makes champagne with them."

The blooms are as sweet as honey, but the leaves smell like dog dirt.

"She makes gallons and gallons of champagne. Cross me heart and hope to die. You should pick some for your mam."

"I'm not allowed in the Dingles," says Cariad.

"Who says?"

"My *mam* says."

Kitty cocks her head to one side. "What's up with her then?"

"She says your sort would as soon steal your purse as look at you."

"Did she now. Well, she won't have much to worry about when we're gone. The council is moving us on."

Where the Dooleys, Coffeys, Driscolls, and Sheridans will be living next God only knows.

"*Arrah*, just go home," says Kitty Dooley. "Miss hoity-toity mammy's baby."

And with that, she gallops off, scaling clumps of nettles and ducking under branches as she goes. Tearing her way through a corridor of weeping willows and disappearing into a tangle of bramble and gorse.

Never to be seen ever again.

Left alone with chattering sparrows and warbling wagtails, Cariad contemplates her life in hell. For after committing a whole *compendium* of sins today, she is surely doomed.

> For if we go on sinning willfully after receiving the
>   knowledge of the truth,
> there no longer remains a sacrifice for sins
> but a terrifying expectation of judgment . . .
>   —Saint Paul, Hebrews 10:26–27

She wonders if elderflowers might lessen the blow when confronted by Biddy. She wonders if whispering the Act of Contrition will cleanse her soul.

"Mea culpa, mea culpa, mea maxima culpa."

As Cariad fills what room she has left in the carrier bag, hoping to gather enough for at least three bottles—no, a *whole bucket* of champagne—a man appears.

A man with a dimpled face.

A man with two buttons for eyes.

The one who stood in the rain on Tixell Road, under an umbrella that was black and vast and wide.

"I see you're having trouble."

He lifts her up. Hoists her high into the air, onto his shoulder.

"There you are. Now you can reach the best ones. The biggest. That's better, eh?"

God doesn't stop the man's hand from crawling up her leg. To her thigh. And further than that. Our Lady doesn't intervene. It's Cariad's will and strength, her very own rage and fury that makes her kick and scream and run like the wind, her carrier bag that's filled with elderflowers, a missal, her veil, and a Holy Spirit locket, clutched tightly to her chest.

•————•

"It's reduced to a rag," says Biddy. "I worked all night, Tom. All night. I didn't sleep a wink, thumbing a beautiful dress together and look at it now. You have a selfish daughter, Tom. Never a thought for anyone else. And what will you do about it? Nothing. Not one iota."

And so Tom dutifully, devotedly, joins in.

Both parents take turns scowling and scolding at the Formica table, in between bites of bread, servings of meat, sips of tea, and spoons of potatoes and peas. With jutting chins and clenching teeth, they recall the times Cariad said this or did that. They rake through bouts of recent misbehavior and compare it with that of the past. They analyze, scrutinize, and debate until Cariad is barely able to distinguish the difference between her rights and wrongs.

And now it's time for Cariad to apologize.

And to promise, from this day on, to be a good girl.
She didn't tell her parents what happened.
She didn't dare.
She claimed Kitty Dooley gave her the elderflowers.
What did Biddy say about tinkers?

•———•

The day Saint Ursula's Convent deems Cariad worthy of their standards is the same day Biddy and Tom put 315 Kingswood Lane up for sale. And three months later, they move fifty miles away, to a town surrounded by orchards, hop fields, and slow rivers. A town where the houses, pubs, and shops are joined at the hip, but where the Catholic church stands small and alone. And the nearest nonpaying school is Brayminster High, where the girls' names are more like Beryl Tudge than Molly Delaney.

•———•

From a young age, I was battered with Catechism, threatened with Hell, and promised a cloud-filled Heaven if I were good. It took several years and Sally Morgan, my new high-school friend, to finally convince me that what happened at the Dingles wasn't God-sent punishment.

Catholic guilt proved to be a destructive burden, difficult to shake off. Its repercussions still affect me to this day, when I least expect it, in ways so subtle, it's rarely easy to identify or recognize.

But it has always offered a wealth of material to write about.

My Counter-Culture Spirituality: How Sudden Death, Tarot Cards, and Mediums Led Me to Quantum Physics—and Belief

Caroline Leavitt

Here I am, six years old, playing with my friend Fay, and both of us are imagining Heaven. Fay decides that Heaven has mansions made out of gold brick. I say that Heaven has all the animals you want, and best of all, I'm not allergic to any of them. My mother wanders in and listens, and then shakes her head. "There's no such thing as Heaven," she says calmly. "God is a myth. All there is after you die are worms and nothingness." Fay looks shocked and I start to cry, but my mother shrugs. "Come in the kitchen and I'll give you a cupcake," she says. "You'll forget all about it."

But I don't forget. Instead, I obsess, lying awake at night too terrified to move, because what if I accidentally fall out of bed, hit my head on the floor, and die, and then the worms get me? My family is Jewish, but no one goes to temple, not even on the High Holidays, but at night I begin to pray to God, stubbornly resisting my mother's teaching. She can be wrong, I tell myself, but deep inside, another voice hisses: *But what if she's right?*

I try not to think about it. I turn twenty, afraid of death. I turn thirty, afraid of death, and then when I'm thirty-two, I fall in love, and though I'm still afraid, happiness tamps the fear down, right up until death enters my life and things suddenly get personal.

I am two weeks away from being married, deliriously happy, planning my life with Steven, a judge who wears an earring and makes me laugh. One night, Steven gets up and says, "I don't feel so well." He's forty-two, healthy, and a runner, and we both think he's just overdone it, but then he sits on the couch and says, "I need to go to the hospital," and before I can get to him, he spills off the sofa, falling to the floor. I run to him and do CPR, but I can't remember how many compressions are needed. I'm hysterically pumping at his chest, breathing into his mouth. I need to call an ambulance, but the phone is in the kitchen. I let go of him and run to the phone, scream for help, and then I race back to him, frantically continuing the CPR, pleading for him to live. The paramedics arrive five minutes later, and as soon as I see them doing the CPR, I know I have been doing it wrong. They're holding his nose. Their compressions are faster. I'm shaking with fear. By the time we get to the hospital, Steven is dead. And so, to all purposes, am I.

I can't eat. I can't sleep. I feel like a layer of life has been ripped from me. One night, after the funeral, I cry in my apartment so loudly a neighbor calls the police, who actually come to the apartment to make sure I'm okay. "I'll never be okay," I tell them. I cry constantly. To friends. To a grief therapist. To my mother, who holds me and strokes my hair, and then tells me, "There is no God. This just proves it."

I can't bear to think that—to imagine Steven buried in the dark without me, without anything. I don't know what to do with myself.

I dream he's alive and a friend tells me, "Maybe he is, on another plane." I scoff, and then I happen to look down, and I see that the crystal of my watch has inexplicably shattered, though I don't remember bumping it on anything. I buy another watch and the same thing happens. In the next two weeks, I buy ten watches, and all the crystals smash. "Could this mean something?" I ask my friend Linda.

"It means you need to buy better watches," she tells me. But my friend Jane says, cautiously, as if she's afraid I'm going to mock her, "Maybe it means something. Maybe it's a message. Maybe you should go to a psychic."

A message! Proof that there is life after death, that there is some force, some God! I'm desperate enough to believe. So I take all the money Steven and I had saved, and I trek across the country, staying with friends. At each location, I find someone to talk to—anyone who might show me God or reason in this tragedy: priests, rabbis, psychics, mediums, palmists, even the waitresses at the diners I frequent.

The religious people are the least helpful. I see a rabbi who hushes me every time I try to speak. "Quiet," he says. "You can talk when I'm finished." I see a priest who tells me that Steven is with Jesus, and I should convert. The psychics aren't much better. I walk into a psychic's house with red eyes as large as kitchen clocks, and the psychic says, "Oh, the spirits tell me you are having your best year yet!" Her smile grows. "Are you pregnant?" she adds excitedly, and I burst into tears.

Then my money runs out and I have to come home, and that's when I read a magazine piece in my shrink's office about a medium. She's college educated. She spent years denying her gift because she was sure it was a brain tumor. There's nothing woo-woo crazy about her photo either. No turban, no flashy earrings. Instead, she looks like a college professor. I call her immediately, and before I can get my name out she says, "Something happened March 8. A man. Dark, curly hair. A heart attack."

She charges $350 an hour—money I no longer really have—but I make an appointment anyway.

Her apartment is filled with antiques, and she sits down and begins to talk, as if we are discussing the weather. She tells me what happened, the how and when of it. She tells me to hire a lawyer because Steven's mother might sue me for his possessions. (I do, and she does.) She tells me that I will be locked out of the apartment because my name isn't on the lease. (It happens.)

"How do you know this?" I ask her, and she tells me that there is no time in the world—that everything is happening all at once. "Read quantum physics," she advises. "Think of it as science we don't know yet."

"So you think there's a God?" I ask. "You really think people are somewhere else after they die?"

She laughs and says, "It doesn't matter what I think. It doesn't change what is." She nods at the door and then says quietly, "You'll see him, but you'll be afraid."

When I leave, I feel so much better. Until an hour later, when I don't.

I want so desperately to believe in something—to give this tragedy meaning—but it still eludes me. If there is a God, I don't like Him because of this cruelty, this torment. I begin to think that if I walked in front of a truck, it might not be so terrible.

A few nights later, I wake to find someone in the room, his back toward me, and it takes me a second to realize it's Steven. He's wearing his favorite jacket, his good sneakers. But instead of being happy, I'm terrified. I run across the hall to stay with a neighbor, and I end up moving in with her for a month. I hate myself for not saying anything to Steven's specter. "It was just a hallucination," my friend soothes, but was it? And even if it was, how did the medium know I'd see him?

I try every way I can think of to find peace. I start writing a new novel. I enter a toxic relationship with a controlling man who won't let me eat, and I stay with him for two years, even promising to marry him, because I know that if I break up, I'll be alone, and the terror and grief will come back. When we do finally split, I give myself some space, and with the help of a therapist and friends, the grief subsides. A few years later, I meet and marry Jeff, a funny, smart journalist, and I get pregnant soon after. I tell myself this happiness is all the meaning I need. I'm too busy to think about God or death. My life is teeming.

And then I deliver Max, a perfect, beautiful boy, and I become critically ill for a year, expected to die. Everything changes again.

I become famous at NYU Medical Center because no one knows what's wrong with me. A kidney failure, they think. Something with my liver. A rare virus they've never seen before. And then they do an operation, and a nurse tells me later that she had never seen so much blood—that it was like something out of *The Shining*, pouring out onto the OR floor. They sew me back up, and my body fills with blood again. None of it is clotting, and they don't know why.

I'm in a medical coma for two weeks, given memory blockers so I won't remember any of it, including any near-death experiences I might have had, which, to be truthful, really pisses me off. What if I had met my own dead loved ones? What if I had seen God Himself? I wouldn't remember. I have five emergency operations, one hundred transfusions a day, and medicines so toxic they will damage my hearing and make me lose my hair.

When I wake up from the coma, there is a woman near me praying. "Everyone knows about you," she says, and she hands me two prayer cards. "God saved you, and these will help you pray to Him," she says, but I'm not so sure, because if God had wanted to save me, why didn't He make me well? Why was I still sick?

She leaves, and I find myself holding the prayer cards tightly in my hand. I don't pray, not exactly, but I say out loud, "I can do this." I mean that I can survive—that I can fight my way back to my husband, my son. I don't know what power is out there—God or positive thinking or the energy of a phrase that becomes my mantra—my way of never ever giving up—but I begin to feel stronger, less panicked. I say the phrase to myself when the ring of doctors comes round and they all talk about mortality rates as if I'm not there. I say it the first time I have to try to walk, after a month in bed, dangerous because it could start another bleed, but my muscles will atrophy if I don't try. "I can do this," I say out loud. "I can do this." And I can.

Three months later, I go home. My family settles back in. I have a baby so new and delicious I want to inhale him! I have a husband who tells me I look beautiful, even with my patchy hair and my swollen, bandaged belly road mapped with surgery scars. Everything looks different to me now. Colors vibrate. I can't believe I'm alive, and I feel different. Changed. As if I've come through something and I want it explained, but again, I don't know where to turn. I wish there were a manual for faith, a set of directions, or even better, a map.

I still have to be in bed for another few months, so I read medical books to figure out why I had this disorder, how it had happened, and most terrifyingly, if it can happen again. And then I remember the medium telling me to read quantum physics, so I order book after book for the layperson.

When the quantum-physics books arrive, they echo what the medium said to me—that the world is stranger than we can imagine and time is man-made, and perhaps everything really is happening at the same moment. I imagine that this is how psychics work, that there is nothing magical about it, that it makes perfect scientific sense. Perhaps they've honed a skill we all have: that is, to dip back and forth in time to pick up thoughts and events, which are energy.

Perhaps it's a gift, like having a talent in singing or art. Maybe a healer is simply manipulating that energy in order to heal, and there's nothing mystical about it at all. The more I read, the more excited I get. There are scientists who believe in parallel universes and think we may have doubles. The one thing I learn from these books—the one piece of information that drumbeats in my head—is that there is so much we don't know about how the universe works, so much we aren't aware of—portals and wormholes and forces and all kinds of amazing things—and couldn't one of these forces be something like God?

When I tell Jeff what I am starting to believe, he sighs. Despite this reaction, I get him to agree that there is a force out there, and we can't know what it is, at least not yet. I don't feel that I'm deluding myself. In fact, the only way I can describe what happened to me because of my experiences with death and psychics is that I now have a feeling, an unshakable sense of *knowing*, much the way people who discover Jesus do, only I don't believe in a Heaven or a Hell, or a God with a beard who judges.

Things begin to make sense to me. Am I fooling myself when I begin to think I survived my illness because I had to raise my son—because *he's* the important one? Am I fooling myself to think I have to write books that reach people, that change them, before I die? And am I fooling myself when I say I don't feel it all ends when our breath stops?

Perhaps you think I'm crazy. That I'm imposing meaning where there is none, because isn't everything random? It doesn't feel that way to me anymore. Of course, I don't know for sure, but I'm going to continue to question, to try to figure this out. Isn't that what science is all about? What I do know is that despite *not* knowing, I'm no longer afraid. I think there is something. And it beats inside of me, just like a heart.

VI

·———·

What I find remarkable is how faith seems to have defined me all along, but I refused to acknowledge its power, whether positive or negative. That harkens back to the child who was never allowed to declare anything hinting of belief and yet was so often filled with the sense of something bigger, greater. Am I talking about God? Some spiritual being that hovers over my life, a universal power that determines (or perhaps even predetermines) the choices I make? I wish I knew. At the same time, is it really so important that I parse my emotions, lay them out to be analyzed and judged? Or might I simply be with them, accept that I feel them, and celebrate the joy of living with a heart more open than it has ever been?

So many of us take the time—in some cases, a lifetime—asking ourselves about faith and how it defines us … or doesn't.

Nothing

Benita (Bonnie) Garvin

Many years ago, a coworker in the theater asked me what religion I was. I told her I was an atheist. She looked astonished, as though she couldn't believe someone she knew and liked was a heathen. With trepidation, she probed me further. "Then what do you believe in?" I replied that I believed in nothing. She insisted I had to believe in something. I explained that my "nothing" was the "something" to which she referred.

Religion is and always has been anathema to me. A tale told to children like the tooth fairy or Santa Claus. I don't believe in god or a spiritual being. I believe life ends with death. To me, my belief seems simple and, from a scientific point of view, accurate. I've intentionally kept myself ignorant about religion. Once I decided to opt for rational thought over religious thought, it seemed pointless to learn the countless practices and symbols people create to convince themselves life is eternal.

I was born into a Jewish family but was an atheist before I even knew what that meant. My parents were Reformed Jews, which is the branch with the most liberal interpretation of the Bible. At eight years old, my goddaughter tried to explain the branches of Judaism to her Christian friend. To the amusement of us all, she innocently described Reformed Jews (like herself and her family) as the "lowest form of Jew."

My parents sent my brother and me to Sunday school. As soon as I started to study the Bible, I knew something was amiss. I loved the stories—particularly those that involved women like Ruth and Esther—but a talking bush and the parting of the Red Sea were among the many stories that aroused my skepticism. I will say, however, that Lot's wife looking back at Gomorrah and turning into a pillar of salt got my attention. I realize many so-called believers don't take these stories literally but rather as metaphors. But metaphors for what? Surely we're all not going to end up on kitchen tables in saltshakers! So what is it supposed to mean?

My parents, particularly my father, thought religion was nonsense, although he tried to keep his opinion to himself. I discovered the truth after I inadvertently overheard an argument between him and my mother. She wanted my brother and me to have a religious identity because, "How would it look if we didn't send our kids to Sunday school?"

I graduated Sunday school and was confirmed, although to this day I have no idea what that means. I know that it didn't require much work, unlike the burden on my poor brother, Larry, who was studying for his bar mitzvah. I always considered my brother the brighter of the two of us and marveled at his ability to learn Hebrew, a language he would immediately discard and have absolutely no occasion to use again. I recall how he withstood several years of torment, studying to become "a man." The arcane idea that a thirteen-year-old becomes a man via a religious ceremony may have seemed logical two thousand years ago, when the average life span was twenty, but not any longer. We're talking about predominately middle-class Jewish kids for whom manhood comes long after the age of thirteen. The only reason I could see my brother putting up with the rigors of his bar mitzvah was the prize money. (My parents "borrowed" the money he received and, as it turns out, never managed to pay it back.)

•———•

When I grew up, my worldview was that people were divided into two groups: Jews and Gentiles. We Jews had been persecuted throughout history and the *goyim* hated us. It was naïve to believe a Jew could ever fully trust anyone other than a Jew. However, there were exceptions. While the overall message was that Jews were superior, my mother made a distinction for New York Jews. For some inexplicable reason, she considered them common and not like the rest of the tribe.

I was obsessed with the division between Jews and Gentiles, particularly as it related to movie stars. I'd quiz my parents ad nauseam as to whether this or that person was Jewish, and was flabbergasted by their ability to look at somebody and know! My mother could even identify when an actress bobbed her nose to hide her true Jewish identity.

I became conscious of subgroups within the Gentile category when a Catholic brother and sister moved in down the street. Unlike my friends and I, who walked or were carpooled to public school, these siblings went to private school, wore uniforms, and rode a school bus. Although I found that unusual, it was the name emblazoned across the side of the bus that sent shivers down my spine: *Precious Blood*. What kind of parents sent their children to a school called Precious Blood? And what unspeakable acts were going on in such a place? For months, after returning from school, I took up residency on the corner, waiting for the arrival of the Precious Blood bus to see if these new neighbors emerged any worse for wear.

•———•

Many of the world's most erudite people, including those I know and respect, believe in god or some religious or spiritual entity. I'm puzzled, because a belief in something so amorphous runs counter to their intellect. For example, when I discovered that the great writer Graham Greene converted, as a grown man, to Catholicism, I lost interest in his books. It's one thing to be raised a Catholic, quite another to convert as an adult. It takes more than a leap of faith to accept wafers as the body of Christ, confessionals, and all the trappings of Catholicism. (And late-life conversions today seem particularly odd, given the heinous abuses that have come to light about the Catholic Church.)

It never occurred to me that I wouldn't marry a Jew. My parents (meaning my mother) were fine with my having non-Jewish friends—provided I didn't spend too much time with them. And until I began high school, I didn't have much exposure to kids who weren't Jewish. But on my first day of high school I became friends with an Armenian. Arlene was pretty and vivacious, plus her father was a doctor, so my mother considered the family refined, the highest compliment she could pay anyone.

Arlene and I were inseparable through our first year of high school. But when we entered our junior year, my mother discouraged our friendship. She feared that spending too much time with Arlene meant I would primarily be exposed to Armenian boys, would abandon Judaism (which I had yet to embrace), and would convert. To what, I didn't know, since I had no clue what Armenians believed!

Throughout college, I clung to the belief that I had to find a Jewish guy to marry. After all, what could I possibly have in common with a man who wasn't one of the Chosen People? I believed the gulf between a non-Jew and me would be so great it could never be bridged, his Gentile culture being as foreign to me as my Jewish culture would be to him. He might order corned beef on white with butter, and I could never grasp or accept the idea of a virgin birth.

Then I fell in love with Jim, an atheist, married him, and was introduced to a new group of Gentiles (what I call the ubiquitous variety). To appease my parents, we were married by an agnostic rabbi. Jim's mother could not have cared less about who performed the ceremony. Her son was marrying a Jew, so what more could go wrong? Although my parents came to love my husband, my mother never failed to remind me, especially when she and I argued, about how tolerant she and my father were of my decision to marry out of the faith. It was as though they'd paid a price for accepting this marriage. (An aunt once told me that when my father was stationed in North Africa and Italy during the Second World War, he became engaged to an Italian woman, the daughter of the town's mayor. When he called to tell his mother, she told him that if he married this Italian Catholic girl, he should never come home. As much as he loved to discuss his time in the army, he never shared that story.)

My parents' hypocrisy is an example of how religion divides people. They welcomed Jim with the caveat of "even if he's a non-Jew" in an effort to show their tolerance, yet never failed to remind me of it. What made it all crazier was that by the time I got married, both of my parents considered themselves nonbelievers. And yet my husband, who didn't consider himself a Christian, was considered one by my parents. Prejudice was never far from their consciousness.

After I'd been married nearly a decade, a woman whom I'd recently met asked me if Jim was Jewish. I replied, "No, he's Gentile." When she asked what *kind* of Gentile—Methodist, Baptist,

Lutheran—my blank look prompted continued probing. "Was he baptized?" she asked. "And if so, into what branch of Christianity?"

I felt like I was taking the SATs again, and I had no idea how to
answer. If she'd held a gun to my head and asked me to define the
differences between the various forms of Christianity, the only thing
I could have told her was how they were spelled. The woman was
gobsmacked, and who could blame her?

I drove home in a state of shock. What kind of person marries
a man without asking about something that most of the "civilized"
world considers fundamental? An hour later, I burst through the door
and confronted my husband. "Jim, what are you?" I demanded, as if
I'd just seen his face on the Ten Most Wanted list at the post office.
He assured me that, like me, he was an atheist, a complete heathen
and proud of it. He reminded me that he had no religious affiliation
or schooling, and that he had never been baptized.

•———•

The majority of wars have been fought in the name of religion. Even
within the smallest of the smallest sects of religions, there is conflict
and animus. I often wonder what would happen if we took religion
out of the picture. Certainly the world would be a more peaceful one.

Growing up, I thought Jews came in three varieties: Orthodox,
Conservative, and Reformed. The majority of American Jews are
Reformed or Conservative. I had never so much as seen an Orthodox Jew until I moved to New York. Once there, I was stunned to
discover that the Orthodox, by far the smallest fraction of the total
Jewish population, had broken up into dozens of subgroups, some
containing as few as a couple dozen people! Ironically, the fact that
they, like other Jews, have been persecuted for their religion doesn't
stop them from rejecting others who don't adhere to their narrow
interpretation of Judaism.

Although religion is purported to build communities and bring people together, we've seen it fuel persecution and hatred. Even the victims of religious persecution have no conflict with turning around and persecuting others. Muslims, Jews, Christians are in religious wars in the name of peace. Indeed, the more fervent the belief, the deeper the suspicion and hatred of others.

Jews declare themselves the Chosen People. Right off the bat, we've sent this message to the world: "The rest of you are, at the very least, second-class citizens." But it's not just Jews who have a notion of superiority. Every religion teaches its followers that they are, theologically speaking, top dog. Therefore, it makes all other religions lesser and drives a wedge between people.

The religious dogma practiced by those who take the Bible literally is a real and present threat to those of us who are rational. We're at a time in our society when religion and science are in direct conflict. Whether in our bedrooms or in our classrooms, many Christians and Muslims are no longer satisfied with practicing their religion in the privacy of their homes, churches, or mosques. They are trying to impose it on the rest of us. They want to tell women what to do with their bodies and gays and lesbians whom to love. What is especially alarming about some Fundamentalist Christians is that they not only believe in the end of days, they're eagerly awaiting them. While the rest of us can barely roll out of bed in the morning, Christ is going to rise from the dead. Why would you seek to reverse climate change if you're looking forward to the Second Coming and the Day of Judgment? Tennessee Republican and self-proclaimed Christian Marsha Blackburn, vice-chair of the House Energy and Commerce Committee, argued during a debate with scientist Bill Nye on NBC's *Meet the Press* that "climate change is still unproven" (Sunday, February 14, 2014).

Whereas evolution was once considered science and taught in public schools, at least a dozen states are now teaching creationism in tandem with evolution—despite the fact that doing so is illegal. A recent poll showed that 80 percent of Americans believe in angels, yet only 25 percent believe in Darwin's theory of evolution![1]

How can we progress if we allow religion to dictate how the social contract is implemented? Medical research using stem cells has been stymied because it offends a particular group of Christians; abortion, although legal in every state, can be obtained in only 13 percent of the counties in America.[2] Such is the influence of religiously oriented antiabortion views.

Our society is held hostage by religion. We give tax credits to religious institutions and their schools. I have no children, but I haven't the slightest resentment about paying school bonds for public schools, and want to do my financial part to help our youth. But the idea that money goes to religious institutions that charge dues and school fees is a direct violation of the Constitution's separation of church and state. Could it be that the lack of outrage stems from a latent fear that if it turns out there is a god, he might be pissed off that we took away his church's tax-exempt status?

No matter what religious affiliation someone professes to be, it is taken more seriously than one's atheism. Even a fringe religion like Scientology, with a belief system inspired by science fiction, and with its pyramid schemes and E-meters, is considered more credible than atheism. I believe that's because atheism threatens the very core belief of most religionists: that life is eternal.

No matter what tribe we're born into—Jewish, Christian, Muslim, etc.—there's a sacred and unspoken bond between us and the other members of the faith. Even when people reject their tribe in an effort to assimilate into another, when the chips are down, old tribal prejudices rear their head.

Many years ago, when I lived in Detroit, I worked for a Jewish man I'll call Murray. Murray possessed the ultimate prize: his beautiful fourth wife was Gentile royalty. Her status came from being the ex-wife of a titan of the automotive industry. Murray took great pride in being the only Jew ever to gain admission to a restricted club. He chummed around exclusively with rich white Christian guys like Lee Iacocca (the man responsible for turning Chrysler around in the 1980s) and people who name their children Flip and Skip and Buffy. Yet when he had something to confide, he had call me, his employee, into his office. Why? Because I was Jewish! After one particularly personal revelation, he remarked, "You know how it is; you're married to a *goy*; it's different with them." It rolled off his tongue without the slightest thought I'd be offended. His assumption was that our respective spouses couldn't possibly understand because they were not Jewish. The man who made me look like a Talmudic scholar was now playing the Jewish solidarity card! His presumptuous assumption was that I would feel as he did—that our membership in the Jewish fraternity trumped all else and this included our loyalties and intimacies with our life partners.

When I was asked to write about faith, the first thought that came to mind was religious faith. Maybe that's because I find that type of faith so troubling. Millions of people around the globe cling to religious faith and doctrine, abandoning reason, logic, and science. They willingly accept that some force or spiritual entity exists without physical proof of its existence. Such belief flies in the face of how the majority of us function in our daily lives. We are, by and large, an inquisitive people. We ask and demand answers about most things. Yet tens of millions of people accept their religion without asking serious questions. The same people who demand to know how many carbs are in their morning cereal or grams of sugar in their can of soda swallow "God works in mysterious ways" as an answer to far more important questions. Imagine your kid coming home after having flunked an exam and running that line on you. And what about all the atrocities that have been committed from the beginning of

time in the name of religion? The Crusades, the Armenian genocide, the Holocaust, to name a few. Isn't it a cop-out to say they also
fall under the "mysterious ways" explanation? If we were honest,
wouldn't we say those events were monstrous, period? And if we
did, wouldn't it undermine the idea of a kind and benevolent being
looking over us? Once we examine one thread, the whole tapestry
begins to unravel. So rather than address this contradiction, "mysterious ways" becomes an easier answer. When I see a *Pray for Peace*
bumper sticker, I always want to ask the driver, "Don't you feel a
little guilty deferring to your god? Given all the people asking for
things, he or she is probably fairly busy. If you care about peace, why
don't you do something about it yourself!"

The evolutionary biologist and author Richard Dawkins points
out that there is no such thing as being born a Muslim or part of any
other religion. A baby doesn't come into this world having weighed
the intellectual and philosophical issues that accompany religion.
It's only as the child develops under the influence of parents and
society that religious affinities develop. It's a mythology created for
and by humans so we can deny the fact that we are mortal and are
going to spend all eternity in the same black nothingness. And as
mortality creeps ever closer, it's not unusual to find somebody like
Graham Greene cramming for finals, just in case he was wrong and
there is a heaven and hell.

There's no way around it: the finality of life is a grim reality.
As Woody Allen said, "the hours are terrible." Somebody recently
asked me how I'd feel if I were wrong and there really were a god.
My answer is that I'd be pleasantly surprised, but it wouldn't change
the standards by which I live my life.

I choose to accept science as it explains life, just as I accept science as it explains the finality of death. Why should one be less valid
than the other? I suspect we don't want to accept science's explanation for the end of life because we don't like the answer.

Sometimes I wish I could wrap myself in the security blanket of religious faith, that I could deceive myself into believing that angels exist, that I will rock out with them in heaven, or even hell, when I arrive for all eternity. But I've lived too long and know too much to deny what is evident when you choose to look: that, regrettably, at the end of life, all there is . . . is nothing.

I'm an Atheist, Thank God!

Malachy McCourt

I am actually a pagan, and this is an antireligion rant.

Organized religion has all the elements of organized crime, except for the lack of compassion. If you offend a crime boss who has no compassion, he will have you beaten up and sometimes killed. If the crime boss wants you to go to hell, he will have you killed after you have committed a sin so you have had no time to repent (i.e., you get yours as you leave a whorehouse or have just eaten pork or have neglected to kill a female relative who has disgraced the family). Organized religion, however, *does* show some compassion. Still, in my mind, crime bosses and the guy called God have a lot in common: revenge, rage, and punishment are essential to their mission.

According to some, God had a son named Jesus Christ. Although the Old Testament says his ancestry goes back to Adam, I've never seen a long-form certificate; I question his birth and his citizenship. The old man sent him off to die for us, and he did not succeed in redeeming us, so he has to come back. I wish he would stay at home and stop bothering us with his comings and goings. One thing we do know is that Jesus Christ could not be president of the United States, as he was not born here. And God was too busy to sleep with Jesus Christ's mother, so he designated a guy called Joseph to stand in for him.

Let's discuss numbers. There are about seven billion people now alive on earth, and about five billion who have died since Adam and Eve started eating apples. This would seem to rule out reincarnation, unless we also return as snakes and Republicans. According to legend, this guy called God created everything and everybody: Saint Francis, Adolf Hitler, Mother Teresa, Jesus, Satan, Muhammad, and Jezebel. It is said that he made man first, from dirt. If he wanted a companion for himself, why didn't he start with a woman? Now we know that, scientifically, if Eve were indeed made out of Adam's rib, she would be 100 percent Adam's DNA. So when he gets in the sack with Eve . . . Well, let's just say that all those lunatics who get upset about same-sex marriage would have a field day.

The amount of time this guy called God spends on the minute affairs of humankind is staggering—everything from sparrows dropping dead to young boys masturbating to exploding atomic bombs to nonbelievers winning the lottery, or whether the Notre Dame football team should triumph over Southern Methodist, or if the New Orleans Saints should be allowed to win the Super Bowl. Very important stuff for this guy to have to decide.

Then there's the matter of who should have been inside the Twin Towers on September 11, and who should have been made late for work and saved. If God is all-powerful, are families examined to determine which children and teachers should be shot in schools across America? People say that this God guy is merciful and compassionate, and simply makes more angels when he has little children killed and moved off this planet. Or (as some have suggested) perhaps these children had sinful parents who couldn't be trusted to bring up the kids to believe in the Lord. And what about the man at the NRA who suggested that God created guns to enable good people to kill bad people? Who gets to decide who is bad?

In our world, we employ people called police officers to prevent bad people from robbing, raping, and assaulting law-abiding citizens. They keep a vigilant eye on known criminals. So if this God guy knows everything, why doesn't he keep an eye on killers—especially child killers—and stop them before they kill? Doesn't legend tell us that God allowed the Romans to kill his own son? Most fathers would gladly take their child's place in the Death Department.

It's amazing to think that God was the world's first landlord and performed the first eviction when he booted Adam and Eve out of the Garden of Eden. And what about his role in capital punishment? There was the small matter of people on earth misbehaving, so was there no better solution than to drown the whole bleeding lot—every man, woman, and child, with the exception of Noah and his family? We're taught that he had to build a ship that would accommodate a male and female of every species, but how can you tell the gender of mosquito without a magnifying glass? I presume elephants, horses, lions, hippopotamuses, hyenas, sheep, tigers, eagles, and vultures were all on board. (There must have been a problem about bringing fish on board, as there was plenty of water outside in the world, so they must have abounded. No point bringing sharks and whales on board, either.) And when you think that there had to be food for all these creatures—but you had to keep the lions from eating the goats—it was no easy task. I suppose they shoveled the shit overboard, although I doubt they had shovels in those days. They also sailed for about 150 days. With Noah being six hundred years old at the time, he must've gotten pretty weary of the whole voyage.

So there we have destruction by a merciful and compassionate God who was so pissed off he flooded the world.

Next came Sodom and Gomorrah, the sinful New Yorks of their day. According to the Bible, the goings-on there were beyond anything that a good person could imagine. So nothing for it but to destroy the two cities and their inhabitants—again every man woman and child—with the exception of a man called Lot, along with his wife, their two daughters, and their boyfriends. But the boys make merry and ignore the girls. One day, the older girl tells her sister she's going to get Daddy drunk that night and let him have his way with her. Where she got the booze is a biblical secret, but bang Daddy she does, announcing to her sister the next morning that she's pregnant. And then she says, "It's your turn tonight," and so Daddy gets drunk again and does what daddies should not do, and the second sister announces the next morning that she, too, is pregnant. And that is how the Lot family continues. Would a compassionate and moral God make people do that?

What about this Tower of Babel? Would building a tall structure actually bring us closer to heaven? And who can prove there's a heaven?

I do not like how religions treat women, although I do understand that we're quick to take fanatical beliefs and apply them to the entire group. We keep repeating that those young Muslims who assemble explosives around their waists and blow themselves up are doing it for Allah, and for their time in Paradise with seventy-two virgins. Would Allah or God really demand that? How compassionate is it to force a girl who's been raped to either marry her rapist or get stoned to death for losing her honor? And what about Orthodox Jewish men who pray, "Thank you, G-d, for not having made me a woman"? I wonder if this God guy is looking down and saying, "Hey, don't mention it!"

One more legend. When King Herod heard from the wise men that a new king had been born among the Jews, he sent out the troops to cut the heads off every male kid two years old and under who lived in the area. I don't see much about that being the fault of Jesus, since he was newly born. Why did all those boys have to die?

Opposing the vicious tide of organized religion is not a task for one human being. I suppose stories about Santa Claus and the tooth fairy and a virgin birth are okay for small children, but when people are taught that some mystical guy in the sky is pulling the strings—and that some people are getting killed and others are doing the killing, and that it's God's will—I don't buy it. When our elected representatives try to convince us that what they are doing is God's work, it's time to go to some other dictatorship. My preference is a people's democracy, not turning power over to some demented cuckoo who wants to either rule or destroy our world. Is it a coincidence that every time the president and many of those miscreants in government intone "God bless America," awful things happen? Plagues, earthquakes, typhoons, tornadoes, floods, terrorism, war—Civil War, World War I, World War II, Korea, Vietnam, Iraq, Afghanistan— and then there's Joseph McCarthy, the election of George W. Bush, depression, disease, the slaughter of schoolchildren. The list goes on . . . and on.

America would be the most blessed country in the world if organized religion were banned . . . and all its agents were sent to Syria.

Faith

Lee Chamberlin

Ontology is the study of being. It explores first principles of our existence and is the purview of metaphysics, where the focus is on subtleties surrounding the workings of the universe. In a world where metaphysics plays a larger role than conventional wisdom is able or willing to acknowledge, faith straddles theoretical explanations of what makes our world and our lives tick, and is the frequent rationale that lends credence to the resolution of situations abandoned as hopeless. Faith fills an emotional and spiritual vacuum.

The Christian Bible deems faith the "substance of things hoped for, evidence of things unseen." At first glance, it appears that to have faith—or more pointedly, to get faith—it is necessary to embrace a codified system of religious precepts. That dictum would compel the irreligious or the merely doubtful to blindly stumble upon a

197

vague and obscure benevolence, somehow willing to make good on all human desires. Much like groping toward a distant, shimmering mirage in a blinding sandstorm.

The Bible further considers one's faith dead if it is without works. It's not enough to say you have faith; you have to do something to prove you've got it tucked firmly under your belt. No idle thumb twiddling or sitting around wishing things were different. The exhortation is to get up, push hard against all seeming odds, and jump into action to prove the intransigence of your belief. You have no choice but to do all you can to actualize the power of something you don't yet have—namely, faith.

The wheel, a metaphysical symbol of life, makes no distinction between the visible and the invisible, the seen and the unseen. Unable to differentiate between life's material-world characteristics and its metaphysical function, the wheel of inevitability sets about its journey to put right whatever is on tilt. The wheel's continuum follows its natural path to restore balance to the dual aspects of the worldly and the spiritual, present in every life. The wheel knows that nothing that occurs is random or without consequence: each and every event is equally important. Every circumstance and every seeming happenstance is valued as an expression of the interconnectedness of all life. It is one's level of belief in the accuracy of the wheel's unavoidable course of correction that is the substance of either blind or enlightened faith.

Enlightened faith presupposes conscious acknowledgement of the wheel's unerring sense of direction to carry us to desired conclusions, despite unanticipated or misleading events. Once the wheel comes full circle, which is unavoidable, all related elements come to light. Ambiguity or assuredness concerning the wheel's path to fulfillment rests in one's resistance or willingness to be led in the direction of limitless possibilities that enlightened or unconditional faith implies. External occurrences may appear to threaten human plans and projections, and deceive us into thinking we screwed up or veered disastrously off course. Before we jump to such conclusions, however, let's consider faith as a power that propels human expectations beyond perceived or foreseeable results. Faith as transcendent.

Ever since we were ushered out of the metaphorical Garden of Eden with no map to show us where to head off to next, conventional wisdom has assumed a confluence of indifferent events and purposeless caprices in perpetual motion, catapulting us through an existence where luck, accident, or coincidence determine the final outcome. If that is so, then what is faith? Where is there room for it? Is faith a good thing, charged with a moral and ethical center, or simply an indiscriminate use of the power of will? And how does anyone who thinks of himself or herself as one of the faith-imbued justify calling on that virtue to commit heinous acts? How does using faith to assist in and justify inflicting injury or violent death on fellow beings square with the Biblically benevolent substance of things hoped for, evidence of things unseen?

• ———— •

Throughout the final years of World War II, a group of Allied soldiers, art historians, and collectors recovered art the Nazis stole from Jews and museums. The Monuments Men, as the group was known, set up temporary art collection points in Europe to protect the stolen treasures they recovered. In early November 2013, the *New York Times* ran a series of articles about the discovery of a trove of valuable art hidden in the Munich apartment of the son of one of a handful of Nazi-sympathizing art dealers charged with selling the looted modernist art to finance Hitler's war efforts.

Among the cache discovered in 2012, and only lately revealed, were some 115 paintings and nineteen drawings registered in the name of the long-deceased dealer. They included works by abstract expressionists Otto Dix, Max Beckmann, Marc Chagall, and George

Grosz, as well as paintings by Gustave Courbet, Pablo Picasso, and
Max Libermann. Some paintings were the works of Dutch masters,
others of Italian and French artists. It was reported that after the
war the dealer had insisted that all of these pieces were registered
in his name and were his rightful property. In 1950, as the art recovery effort was winding down, the treasured works were returned to
the dealer.

Following the war, and absent today's sophisticated data-
tracking technology, returning stolen art works to their original
owners proved difficult. However, a contemporary database not
only led to the hidden treasures but confirmed that at least eight
of the paintings falsely declared by the dealer to be his were, in
fact, stolen by the Nazi regime. So far, only one painting among
more than 1400 newly unearthed canvasses and drawings has found
its rightful owner. The granddaughter of a well-known French
art dealer of the pre- and postwar periods confirmed a recovered
painting by Henri Matisse as having belonged to her family. A
black-and-white photograph of the original was all that remained
in her family's archives of purloined art. At the end of sixty-three
years, one family's loss was set right.

With justice served—and heaven's first rule of order restored—
we are free to entertain the possibility of blind faith. Without the
opportunity to speak with the granddaughter about her hopes for
restitution of cherished family property, we are at liberty to consider
the wheel's circle of completion.

•———•

Some seventeen years ago, my closest friend was diagnosed with
lymphatic cancer. The recommended chemotherapy treatment
involved bimonthly hospital visits over a period of several months.
During the early sessions, we held hands and watched together as
the rose-colored chemical fluid flowed down a clear plastic tube

into her arm. On many occasions, especially during the accumu-
lated hours spent driving to and from the hospital, she and I spoke
of things material and spiritual—of events rationally inexplicable
or singularly phenomenal that caught our attention. From her comments, her faith in a benevolent, all-seeing, all-caring, all-powerful
God was made clear.

After months of these biweekly chemotherapy treatments, her
son learned of an alternative therapy she and her family felt might
better serve her recovery. To this end, the two of us traveled from
Southern California, where we lived at the time, to the alternative
therapy clinic in Mexico, where she began a supervised two-week
inpatient protocol. I stayed with her the first week; her dad did the
honors week two.

Her father and I understood that to continue the therapy at
home, she would need assistance from someone fully invested in the
value and efficacy of its healing process, and mentally and physically equal to the task. When a cancer patient is enfeebled by the
disease, as she was, or slowed down by surgery, the therapy is nearly
impossible to pull off alone. Full participation to insure success calls
for stamina, limitless patience, and a strong measure of understanding from everyone involved. Above all, she would need patience to
complete the eighteen- to twenty-four-month-advised time period
necessary to restore her severely compromised immune system. The
therapy could not be rushed, especially in her case of an extremely
invasive cancer. Once the therapy was complete, the damaged body
would be again fully equipped to heal itself. In spite of the challenge ahead, her father and I agreed on the impressive results we
witnessed at the clinic and the progress she made during her stay. It
was a hopeful, if anxious, time for us all.

A short while after leaving the clinic, her original oncologist
examined the diseased lymph nodes in her neck and shoulders by
applying finger pressure to the area. He was surprised to discover the

nodes no longer swollen but normal in size, and pronounced the cancer gone. Fortified by this news, she attended a large faith-healing gathering led by a popular television personality, who singled her out as "someone in the audience" recently faced with a life-threatening disease who was now cured. He pointed to where she sat in the crowded auditorium. Encouraged, she decided to put her faith in the healer's word as confirmation of the oncologist's recent finding and discontinued the alternative therapy at home. A few weeks later, the oncologist's same finger-pressure examination revealed that nodes, previously returned to normal size, were again swollen. The cancer had recurred.

Everything changed. An awkward, unfamiliar distance set in between us. She withdrew into thoughts she no longer shared with me, slept a good deal, and like an obedient child, dutifully swallowed the oncologist's prescribed medications. The buoyant talks that filled our days with wonder over singularly phenomenal and rationally inexplicable solutions to problems in our lives (and in the lives of others we knew) ended. Something within her proved unable to recover a principle on which she had built a belief system that sustained her up to and including the onset of her illness. I asked if with the new diagnosis and the healer's confident recovery claim, she felt betrayed. A hard silence and dark, uncompromisingly defiant eyes were my answer.

No matter how long I spent attempting to convince her to continue to hope, or how relentlessly I pressed arguments about beliefs that had carried her through many difficult personal trials of the past, the light in her eyes was gone. She listened to me with polite, if strained, patience as I rattled on, but it was clear she had given up on any hope of rescue from the all-seeing, all-caring, all-powerful God on whose benevolence she had once relied with unqualified certainty. Without faith in her God, she seemed to lose every reason to go on. She was listless and submissive. She did ask me to continue to visit and sit with her, but not to talk. She wanted my company but not my cheerleading. Some weeks later, she closed her eyes and slipped away. At her hospital bedside sat her ex-husband, a man she had loved deeply and in whom she had trusted, but who had betrayed that trust.

• ———— •

One morning, six months prior to this writing, I awoke to discover the area from under my breasts to just above my pelvis to be unnaturally distended—I looked four months pregnant. I was not in pain but quite uncomfortable, physically and mentally. I was not frightened.

Over the years, I've come to recognize that every adversity or challenge has led to unexpected good. My beliefs and the spiritual path I follow help me not to fear death of the body. On a three-week summer vacation with my son and his family, and far from home in an unfamiliar part of the country, I had no idea where to begin the search for a doctor. I believed I was in the grip of nothing more than a bad case of constipation, hardly reason to dial a doctor, yet the distension persisted for several weeks and resisted every over-the-counter remedy I tried. Finally and reluctantly, I agreed to consult a primary-care physician. With her thorough examination complete, she ordered an immediate CT scan and referred me to an oncological-gynecological surgeon. The scan and the oncologist's exam confirmed both medical opinions: the presence of cancer in my uterus was causing the bloating, the urinary-tract infection, and the weight loss. They believed that the malignancy was confined within the uterine walls and had not spread to other organs.

Ten days later, the surgeon performed a total hysterectomy, removing my uterus (where the cancer had localized), as well as my ovaries, cervix, and fallopian tubes, although lab tests confirmed these organs were cancer free. When she and I discussed the rationale behind such a radical medical procedure, she first noted that I was her "healthiest patient." She went on to explain that although early detection had enabled her to successfully "remove all the cancer" and none was indicated in those organs deemed cancer free, her caveat included the possibility of remaining cancer cells in the far reaches of the bladder, undetectable to the naked eye. She recommended a post-surgery recovery period of eight weeks before beginning biweekly chemotherapy sessions. Each would last four hours, extended over a period of six months, and they were, in her opinion, the most effective preventive measure. I strongly disagreed.

Among several reasons for dismissing her therapeutic suggestion as workable for me was her inability to offer any guarantees that such an extreme method of scattershot prevention would yield satisfactory results. I also considered an additional six-month imposition on my son's young family—I would be staying in their home during treatment—to be far more support than they could or should be asked to shoulder.

For an organic foodie and vegetarian of thirty years' duration, a nonsmoker and not much of a drinker, a woman who jogs two miles, three times a week, and who a few years earlier, ran a 26.2-mile marathon, I wondered how an oncologist's "healthiest patient" got sick. My thoughts traveled back seventeen years, when I had played a relatively minor role as observer, confidante, and facilitator for a very dear friend in a similar situation. Hard to ignore the wheel's full circle.

The moment had arrived to take stock of a good deal more than the physical aspect of my life. "Healthiest patient" or not, my mind-body-spirit connection was on *tilt*.

In the event that traces of the malignancy lurked in my bladder as suggested, I rethought what I believed to be the best means and the best time to begin preventive therapy. I didn't consider it a good idea to wait eight weeks to give the theoretical bad cells a head start to develop and once again take charge. It seemed a better idea to rebuild my body weakened by surgery and cancerous tissue as quickly, as informed, and as wisely as possible. It was up to me to get a firm grip on my life and my recovery process. I read up on therapies other than chemo that proved successful in helping cancer patients get back on solid ground. I discovered documented ways to restore health and combat undetected or undetectable disease. I learned that juicing certain raw vegetables is most effective for the body to quickly and easily absorb the vitamins, minerals, and enzymes a compromised immune system lacks. Based on the narratives I read, I plunged full-out into a daily, self-prescribed regimen of frequent juicing of organically grown carrots, celery, and beets. I eliminated foods containing fat, sugar, or salt—all known to stimulate the growth of latent and active cancer cells. I practiced visualizations of my thinner body as fully restored to its previous appropriate weight. Every day I loudly and enthusiastically repeated positive affirmations of a new, improved, healthier physical, mental, and spiritual self, got plenty of bed rest, and avoided lifting anything over ten pounds.

•————•

Two years before the cancer diagnosis, I had established an American-based, theater-oriented nonprofit organization whose theater activities were to take place partly in France, partly in the United States. Before leaving America to move to France, I sold or gave away nearly everything I owned, placed my books and art work in storage to be claimed later, and crammed the rest of my belongings into four suitcases. I was on my way back to Paris, this time to live permanently, and fully committed to lending substance to a long-held dream.

After relocating from a temporary living arrangement in a friend's unoccupied Paris apartment, I followed what I took to be the sound counsel of a French friend who advised that the best city for my organization's theater work was a university town some two

hundred miles southwest of Paris. I moved from the City of Light
to what turned out to be a provincial enclave, where strong ties
of childhood friendships and impenetrable bonds of tightly knit,
tradition-bound families are not inclined to open arms to newcom-
ers (defined as anyone whose local family history does not date
back at least six generations). A medium-sized metropolis that
shuts down at eight in the evening on weekdays (and barely opens
at all on Sundays) proved less than ideal for a native of the Big
Apple—a city that never, ever sleeps, and where everybody is welcome. My social life narrowed to chatting with my organic-food
grocer or exchanging pleasantries with the newspaper vendor. Telephone visits with distant family, faraway friends, and friends in
not-so-far-away Paris did little to ease the soul-crushing solitude
and grinding boredom. Shallow, stressful sleep and daily headaches
outpaced all the benefits of my organic-food diet, jogging regimen,
and brave exterior. I was deep in the dumps and very much alone.

• ———— •

At the end of twenty isolated, dispiriting months, a sadness over-
shadowed my daily life that was so profound it prompted a Parisian
friend to mention she'd never seen me look or sound so sad. I lacked
the courage to acknowledge that I was ready to throw in the sponge
and disappoint a lot of people, including myself. It was impossible
to admit that my desire to continue to live and work in Europe was
shrinking, but I had no idea where I wanted to land if I returned to
the States.

I moved from the provinces back to Paris, this time into my
own apartment: it wasn't enough. The challenge still lay in fulfilling
the expectations of my organization's start-up donors and meeting
my own lofty expectations based on a fervent belief in the project's value, which was substantiated by a winning breakout season.
Before long, the growing, ever-present financial concerns overshad-

owed our successful debut. Endless funding shortfalls prodded me to doggedly coax the organization up a path rutted with more downs than ups. There was a blurred distinction between who I was and what I was attempting to do. *I* became the organization. I conflated my identity as a theater artist with the shortcomings and critical condition common to all fledgling projects. Anxiety and loneliness had worn me down. My immune system was compromised.

•————•

Seventeen years ago, the only way to take advantage of the alternative clinic's therapy was to travel to Mexico as an inpatient. Today, a simple log-on gains access to streamed workshops and printed materials for step-by-step guidance and details of the medical research that informs the course of treatment. I had no exterior or interior cancerous tumors. I was relatively healthy, rapidly regaining post-surgery physical and mental strength, and feeling confident of my ability to manage the exacting protocol without help. I logged on, signed up, and fully embraced the alternative.

Several months have passed since then. I feel physically, mentally, and spiritually healthier than I've ever felt. My faith in the therapy's recovery record and protocol, coupled with the decision to actively participate in my healing, awards me a new lease on life. I regard this unavoidable detour as an opportunity to evaluate and incorporate the interconnectedness of all the compartments of my life. Introspection and a determination to understand what went wrong cast light on the many reasons for the dark days of a clouded mind, hobbled spirit, and sickened body. I face fears head-on, keep a discriminating eye on thought patterns, review and define new ways to accomplish my goals. I daily affirm that I am not what I do.

Ontology is as valid an approach to the means to reconfigure purpose and meaning of existence as any other hypothesis. In the study of being, and in the attempt to unveil the universe's mysteries, faith in oneself can foster acceptance of the presence of guiding forces inexplicable by logic or reason. Faith can harness belief systems that consider the wheel a determinant to consequences of human behavior. Seventeen years ago, I was drawn to a healing place I knew nothing about yet proved instrumental in helping me save my life. Faith and the wheel are full of surprises.

VII

•——————•

Where I once existed on the cold, hard tundra of agnosticism, I find myself stepping into rich and arable earth. Does it frighten me? A bit, yes. Will that fear stop my journey? No, I've traveled too far and with too much heart.

The leap of faith I've taken—and continue to take—fills me with wonder. I'm the woman who has avoided the subject of faith and belief for nearly seventy years. Yet here I am, discussing it until some friends' eyes nearly roll back; probing into questions of faith while I slide back and forth on my rowing machine; waking up to these questions at three in the morning and wondering why I've taken this path; asking myself, sometimes uneasily, where it will lead; and then mustering the courage (or is it foolishness?) to share my feelings with readers who can only judge me by what they read. For whatever reason (if reason plays a role at all), I find myself thinking about faith and my beliefs as I write, edit, teach, spend time with my grandchildren, drive my car; I am poking into dark spaces, wondering how, as I've moved through stages of my life, I've managed to avoid taking note of seismic shifts in faith—yet avoidance has been my aim. Experiencing the deaths of friends and friends' children, of my parents, of a beloved friend in Amsterdam, and then forging ahead, ever stoic, as if all were fine, as if nothing had changed. Wanting to believe in something that gave me strength as a child; afraid to believe in the same as an adult. And today, again wanting to believe, secure that I now have the confidence and the wisdom to push aside my resistance and jump in, yet still uncertain. Uncertain . . . and enthralled.

Good, God-Fearing Atheist

Jacquelyn Mitchard

When my daughters Merit and Marta came to the United States from Ethiopia, they prayed their grace before every meal in their native language, Amharic.

It was a beautiful prayer that sounded something like this: *Nishala kishala mishala alia shalla.* . . . It went for long moments, and seeing sweet five-year-old Marta lisp out those words with her huge eyes slightly lidded was a humbling, deeply moving sight. All of us gathered around the table felt we should pray also, but we didn't have the custom of it. Still, we bent our heads and listened to Marta's voice, loving her all the more.

When Marta spoke to her dying birth mother in those months, she later said that her mom had reminded her that I must take them to "God's house."

I knew what she meant.

In their homeland, the constant of my daughters' lives had been daily church—right through their slide from the nether edges of the middle class after Dad died from AIDS, to Mom's sickness, to the orphanage. They were devout Ethiopian Orthodox, and I sometimes think that if I were a person worthy of them, I would have found a way to continue the tradition of their early childhood, which so sustained them. Instead, I took refuge in hippie (albeit Emersonian) existential platitudes: God is all around you, in the storms and in the sea. God is in the face of those you love.

My daughters don't remember those prayers anymore.

We are indeed a family who sits down together each night for dinner, but we don't pray. "God's house" is the place at the end of the street, where you turn around when you're giving the dog his walk.

We're not religious.

Yet I am not fooling when I tell you that I really wish I could find that small coal within myself and fan it into a flame.

I'm sorry that I'm an atheist.

It embarrasses me.

I don't know why.

Perhaps it's because I feel as though I'm letting people down. My children. My friends. Perfect strangers.

I don't feel as though I'm missing anything.

I'm not unhappy to have the conviction that our lives are a brief space of light between two vast darknesses—that it is in the shelter of each other that we find our sustenance. I am not ashamed to share the belief of Abraham Lincoln—that Christianity is a mortal construction.

I don't yearn for a world to come. Mightily as I miss the people who have died—my brother, my mother, my husband—I don't expect ever to see them again, except in the sweet well of my memory.

People say I'm cheating myself; they say they'll pray for me. They tell me that I don't get what it's like to "know" Jesus personally. They're right. I absolutely do not—and in truth, I don't think they do either.

Perhaps there's a genetic predisposition to welcoming religious faith, as there is to alcoholism.

We're all born innocent, without a belief in anything except those around us (who, if we're lucky, shelter and nurture us). Belief in a God—or in anything unseen—is a learned behavior. People assure me that angels exist. They assure me that they see ghosts. I believe that they believe that they're telling the truth. But I don't believe in ghosts or angels any more than I believe in God.

Did I say that I wish I did? It would be kind of lovely and wonderful. I do not, though, hard as I've tried.

Although God was frequently invoked or called upon in our sometimes-Catholic, sometimes-Anglican home, in supplication or in vain, God as the giver and the redeemer and the judge was never really a presence. Before middle school, like all my friends, I saw the Hayley Mills movie *The Trouble with Angels* and became obsessed with being a nun, reading about nuns, wearing the cool outfit—living in a world with definite rules, uncomplicated by the vicissitudes of boys and career choices. Then in high school, I read the Bible through, twice, loving the language and the stories.

But that small coal never ignited.

Even if you have no genetic predisposition, certainly you need an emotional predisposition—the kind people have who fall in love at first sight. They can ignore how complex love turns out to be.

If you live through faith, you can ignore how God gets the credit for all things good, and human beings get the blame for all things bad. You're not supposed to recoil from being a craven supplicant, constantly beating your breast ("through my fault, through my fault, through my so-grave fault . . ."), even when having a sharp tongue and accidentally stealing a hotel hair dryer ("it looked just like mine") are the sum of your sins. You're supposed to be able to prostrate yourself at the feet of a god who, despite your devotion, considers you as unworthy as you consider yourself.

None of this made any sense to me as a child. And it makes no more sense now.

Matters of the spirit don't have to make sense. They aren't subject to temporal standards. Yet the all-purpose rejoinder "you take it on faith" sounds soppy to me. I reserve the right to expect the practices I endorse to be scaffolded on at least some form of logic.

Still, despite all this, I did try to take my children to church when they were little, because I wanted them to be part of a community, or something, especially after I was widowed. It didn't work out, though. Like so many other things, it seems that the emotional propulsion for religious observance must come from the parents, and I just wasn't feeling it.

Sporadically, I've been inspired to try again.

Ironically, it was the friends who are religious who didn't help.

I know that my failure to believe makes them uncomfortable, just as it makes people uncomfortable that I don't drink, although I'm not an alcoholic.

While my friends are nothing like the "clerical bullies" that the late and acerbic Christopher Hitchens so railed against, they do offer opinions that ruffle my feathers.

Here are some of them.

"Don't you think your kids need a . . . moral structure?"

Of course I do, and I also think that the most successful structure parents can communicate comes from example. But that answer makes me sound like a ninny who considers herself a flawless being—which I don't. I just don't need a deity to help me teach my kids right from wrong.

"Don't you . . . need something to believe in?"

Yikes! Absolutely! And there are plenty of things I do believe in—justice, acceptance, charity, human kindness. I don't believe that good character emanates from a deity, though the Judeo-Christian ethic is a perfectly good way of living.

"Have you tried opening your heart?"

Yes. Newly widowed, I remember coming alone into the quiet house, paying the sitter, taking off my shoes, hanging my coat in the closet and then, concentrating every neuron, whispering, "God, here I am, your child. Please be with me." But there was nothing in the hall except me, a lonely young woman with wet hair and no money, shaking out her umbrella and trudging upward to the bedroom.

"Don't you think that some exposure to values will help prevent your children from getting in trouble down the road?"

Why, yes, I do.

Not long ago, I was at a dinner with seven or eight professionals and well-heeled stay-at-home moms. All of us had teenage children. One of the women was a defense lawyer. At the end of the meal, she passed out her business card. I smiled but didn't take one, and she noticed. "Oh," she said. "Don't think you'll be needing me, huh? These folks know better."

I'm not enough of a fool to think that none of my kids will ever get in trouble with the law. One already did—years ago, when stopped for a broken taillight, he learned he had six hundred dollars worth of jacked-up parking tickets. It was the Friday after Thanksgiving, and the judge wouldn't be in until Monday. Our hearts breaking, in tears, we let our son sit in the Rock County Jail for two days. Do you think Yahweh could have been sterner? Probably that was too stern (as the firstborn, he gets all the travail). Friends said some things are more important than principles. But is anything really more important? Principles let you live within the group, prosper, be loved, and share in the good things.

That impulse, to be good and do good, comes from God.

No, that impulse comes from self-preservation.

I suppose I could have a conversion experience born of hard times. But I've had very hard times—losing my parents young, witnessing my father's abuse of my mom, the death of my husband, losing all my money, multiple losses of pregnancy—and they haven't yet changed my mind.

Now, don't be misled by thinking that it was bitterness over God's reaction time in consoling me over these and a dozen other concussions that kept me from giving myself to faith. I'm not even cynical. I probably never had what Quakers called "that of God" within me, although a Quaker meeting was the only form of religious gathering I ever enjoyed. I never felt the call to prayer, although at times I am deeply, *deeply* superstitious, calling on the saints of my youth—especially Saint Anthony and Saint Francis de Sales—because saints at least knew what it was like to be human.

It would also be unfair to say that I don't think being religious is weird. I think it's as weird that people believe as they think it's weird that I don't. I want them to change. I don't go to atheist rallies to try to get God taken out of the oath of office or the Pledge of Allegiance. Even if I don't think it belongs there, I also don't think it really means what it says exactly, any more than it would be a statement of faith if the newly elected said, "So help me, Hannah."

And if I got proof, I certainly would believe. If I saw a ghost, I would revise my opinion on ghosts. In fact, I routinely contrive to stay in places that sane people swear are haunted, and I experience nothing; I guess I am a ghostbuster. I tell my friends I'd actually like to experience a middle-level haunting. Several shudder. They say, indeed, I have no idea what I'm talking about (they're correct). Two have had the same experience in an old building where we all stayed. They tell me about an invisible being that hovered above them at the level of the ceiling, then swooped down and pressed on them, lay beside them. My question was . . . why? Why would a ghost do something so goofy, even if the ghost were real?

Where's the proof that they weren't just dreaming? Proof does not seem unreasonable. Even if you can't prove something does not exist, you should be able to prove something does.

You might say, "Well, I believe what I believe, and I don't need proof." Yet, as a magazine piece recently suggested, no one would have trusted Jonas Salk if he had simply said he "believed" that the polio vaccine would be effective.

Perhaps the most compelling of all the reasons I don't believe, however, is that God's mercy (like the wrath of Him) seems so darned random.

A woman who worked for me once told me that I could live my life doing good works and never harm a living soul, but unless I accepted Jesus Christ as my personal savior, I could not enter heaven. She told my then five-year-old daughter the same thing: it was incumbent upon her as a fundamentalist Christian to share the "good news," which was not particularly good news to my little girl, who cried to think of her mommy burning in hell.

My child said, "God loved us so much He gave his little baby up to die to save the world. Would you give me up to save the world?"

"Absolutely not," I told her. "The whole world could be reduced to ashes before I'd harm a hair on your head."

What kind of hokum is this?

God seems always to be asking the faithful to tear up their clothes, live at the dump, let their kids be stricken with plagues, even kill their own children as proof of their loyalty. (Although the Lord changed his mind at the last minute—do you think Isaac needed therapy for trust issues thereafter?) God asks this in the promise that the most excoriated (Job springs to mind) will receive greater blessings than those less sorely punished.

My question is this: Who is so self-seeking he would allow his family to be destroyed, or kill his own child, in the hope of greater blessings *for himself*? Do you want to be part of that club?

Not long ago, a beloved relative explained that she believed she had a guardian angel. (She had also had several drinks at the time.) She related how, one day, she was driving to the mall when something "just told her" to turn around and go the other way. Inevitably, there was a huge motor-vehicle pileup with multiple fatalities. "And I would have been one," she said.

Several years ago, a woman both of us knew well, one of the best friends I ever had, suffered what was apparently a strep infection that went systemic when it was untreated. She was driving (to my house, actually, with her toddler in the car) when she had what doctors think was a heart attack. Taken by ambulance to the hospital, she was successfully revived but never regained consciousness. A healthy woman in her forties, she remained in a coma for three years, her parents and her husband, all cradle Catholics, as well as most of her friends, prayed for a miracle—even when physicians told them that Stacey would never, ever speak or think again. There was no activity in her brain above the brainstem. Finally, mercifully, one morning when I was alone with her at the beautiful hospice facility where she was finally moved, she died.

Stacey was no saint, but she was an extraordinarily good and genuine person, loving and beloved, funny and honest, gentle and steadfast.

The evening of her death, I said to my relative, "What about Stacey? Why didn't she have a guardian angel?"

And this relative, who also is an excellent and good person, said, "She just didn't."

That was okay with my relative.

But it's not okay with me.

If God's that much of a whack job and all we get to say is, "Well, He works in mysterious ways," you can have God and all the trimmings. The whole premise feels faulty and, to get my vote, God would have to be at least explainable, at least thoughtful and precise, rather than haphazard and cruel.

So I remain a person who examines her conscience every day and calls herself to task—what you might call a good, God-fearing atheist. And I'm sticking to it, so help me, Hannah.

Faith: A Personal Journey

Mara Purl

My grandfather passed away when I was three years old. I was holding his hand at the time, sitting on my tiny chair with my arm stretched up to reach his. I often sat there during his final illness, reading to him the stories in my picture books. I had no fear when he died because I had no sense of loss. I knew with a child's absolute certainty that he was just as fine as he had been a moment before, because his life was continuing. When my grandmother came into the room a few moments later, she gasped, realizing he was gone. "It's okay, Mamaw," I told her. "He's with God now."

Where this certainty came from, I don't know. I do know it gradually waned through the years, and I began to marvel at how I had ever felt so positive about the continuation of life and the existence of a beneficent Guide, particularly since I wasn't born into a religious family. The few times I attended a Sunday school during childhood were at my own request, as my parents had no church affiliation nor any noticeable spiritual leanings. Through my early teen years, I found myself *wanting* to trust that inner guidance yet worried that I might find myself leaning on something ephemeral. Thus began my quest to gain, in a grown-up sense, the certainty I'd felt so early.

While I was still a child, my family moved to Japan for my father's business career. For the next several years, I attended an international school, and was exposed to more than forty different nationalities and cultures. The cafeteria was a microcosm for the world: for the Catholics, fish on Friday; for the Hindus, vegetarian offerings; for the Jews, kosher selections; for the Chinese, an omnivorous selection of meats and sauces. Since everyone eating these meals was a friend or schoolmate, it seemed perfectly natural to me that life included such variety.

Meanwhile, beyond the walls of school and home, my sister and I enjoyed daily interaction with the dynamic multilayers of Tokyo, a fast-paced, sleekly modern city overlaying one of the world's most ancient cultures. The secular predominated daily business life. But personal and family rituals all centered around not one but two religions that fit together compatibly, like two halves of a spiritual puzzle.

One religion was Shinto, which appeared to a noninitiate child foreigner to be a joyful, polytheistic series of rituals to mark every important occasion in life—be it New Year's Day, when a million people would press themselves through the Meiji Shrine in the middle of the city, or the opening of a business, when huge floral medallions would be leaned against the doors of the new establishment.

The other was Buddhism, which seemed swathed in mystery. This religion, by contrast, focused on a quiet oneness—a solemn stillness that only a devotee with a shaved head and a monk's robe could practice. Curiosity and educational field trips led me to visit many temples, and each time I did, the multiple images of the Buddha—from the gigantic statue in Kamakura to the hundreds of sculpted images in Kyoto to the tiniest reproductions in tourist shops—seemed to contain secrets locked within an enigma.

My family also traveled to several other countries, and while we were in India, I found myself intrigued by yoga, which became a deeper study. From a spiritual perspective, what I learned from this ancient faith (and from reading about the advanced yogis and their practices) is that all things are possible for the mind that comes unstuck from a preoccupation with matter and with material circumstances. I glimpsed what physicists have since been proving—that matter itself is more of a collective agreement than an unbreakable set of laws, more a reflection of our thoughts than the framework of our universe. And I began to learn that meditation can break limitations and open vistas unavailable to the physical senses.

Halfway through high school, I was sent back to the States to attend an Episcopal boarding school, where I had my next exposure to Christianity, which I found troubling. Each day began with a morning assembly and the singing of hymns—for me, unaccustomed rituals. And though two devout and very dear priests came to my new school to conduct evening prayers, I couldn't seem to grasp the essence of their message.

What I had learned from Japanese culture was a sense of discipline that was both individual and collective. One behaved a certain way in public because one was representing not only one's self but also one's culture. In my case—as a foreigner whose coloring and height made it impossible to blend in—I was representing America writ large wherever I went. What the Christian religion of my boarding school was instructing, however, was that one could make a mistake, apologize, and affect some kind of contrition. Then one was free to repeat the offence. I just couldn't respect a religion that offered excuses rather than responsibility. It wasn't until I was graduating from college that I discovered a truer sense of forgiveness and acceptance, some of the keys at the heart of the Christian message.

It was then that spirituality, rather than religion, began to percolate in my life as a sometimes uncomfortable but wonderfully enlivening series of experiences. Synchronicity was the first "symptom" of this evolving consciousness, and I had several consecutive experiences when I'd think of someone and they'd suddenly appear. The most outstanding example was when I found myself thinking about a friend from Ghana, and to my amazement, he showed up at the door of my college dormitory.

The next "symptom" was even more vivid. Not feeling well, I visited the infirmary and was diagnosed with mononucleosis. Since I was excused from classes, I spent a week meditating and journaling in my dorm room. I reached out for that Presence that I'd felt as a child and suddenly began to link together my various chapters of religious investigation—until I recognized them as an ongoing spiritual path on which I'd already been traveling. This seemed to be the next chapter, and I was more curious than ever, more open to new possibilities. At last I began to be able to slough off the nagging skepticism and feel the beginning of trust. I was touching the edge of faith.

The result was startling. A week after that diagnosis, I returned to the infirmary and requested a new test. At first they refused. Eventually, they relented and all traces of the disease were gone. This was officially recorded as a mistake, but I knew in my heart of hearts that this was no error. I knew something had *happened*. What, exactly, I didn't know. But with every cell and fiber, I knew I'd had an experience beyond personal will and self: a spiritual experience.

During my week of solitude, I'd begun a special journal. I still have it, a large burgundy, cloth-bound volume with unlined pages— the kind of blank notebook one might purchase for sketching. In it I'd begun to chronicle this new chapter, where *thoughts* seemed to become *things* in the metaphysical blink of an eye. Now I began transcribing phrases and sentences, notions plucked from a more rarified air than the intellectual or emotional musings I'd previously recorded. As page after page filled with these unusual ideas, I began to crave confirmation that others might have had a similar experience. Yet when I dared to mention some of the ideas I'd written in my journal to a classmate, she appeared startled, then disturbed.

I later discovered that the source of her disturbance was several phrases and ideas I'd shared with her. These were, in fact, ideas she'd studied all her life. Born into a religious family, she and her parents were devout students of a religion founded by an American woman in the 1800s. Yet my friend abhorred proselytizing and feared to mention how closely our thoughts now apparently aligned. When she'd withdrawn, she'd done so to pray about what to do. At one point during my earlier investigations I'd studied the *I Ching*, and it suddenly occurred to me that she might find it interesting. I left a copy of it in her mailbox with a note tucked inside. This was the signal she'd been waiting for, and after an absence of a few weeks, she responded with a gift: a copy of a book called *Science and Health with Key to the Scriptures*.

I began reading this paperback immediately, speeding through it as voraciously as I might a juicy novel. Each time I came across the word *Christian*, I was put off. Yet the rest of the text made so much sense that I felt compelled to keep reading. Imagine my amazement when I began discovering phrases I'd previously written in my journal! Two examples that stick in my memory are "thought expands into expression" and "causation is mental."[1]

I'd signed up to take the Graduate Record Exams (GREs) at Harvard, and my friend invited me to stay that weekend with her parents, who lived in Boston. She'd driven with me from our college in Vermont, and that first evening, her folks hosted a wonderful dinner for us, which included a family friend also visiting from out of town. My classmate and I both came from entertainment families, and stories around the dinner table were hilarious and familiar. What I found so curious, though, was that both her parents and their other guest—each of whom had major credits to their names—had all left the business to become practitioners who helped people have healings. I must have been their most persistent and obnoxious guest, as I peppered them with questions, yet they seemed to welcome my inquisitiveness and answered with candor.

Twenty-four hours later, after an eight-hour day of grueling exam questions, I arrived back at their apartment with a headache. I excused myself after a quick dinner to lie down in the guest room, but by a couple of hours later, the headache had progressed to a migraine. I asked if they had any medication and was stunned when they replied that they had none. By then, all stores were closed. I spent the night using breathing techniques, yoga headstands, and anything else I could think of to ease my discomfort, without much success. In the morning I asked my friend's mother what *they* did for headaches. "We study, pray, and listen," she said.

"Well, can you do whatever you do when you help people?"

She agreed immediately.

I don't remember much about what she said during the half-hour meeting we had that morning. She referred to *Science and Health* and assured me I could have one of these healings I'd heard about. My friend and I then had to pack up and head back to school. As we were about to drive off, her mother leaned into my car and said, "Remember, you're perfect!"

That bizarre statement worked through my brain all during our three-hour drive back to Vermont. I found myself arguing with it. *Perfect? Me?! Of course I'm not perfect! Nothing could be further from the truth!* On and on the argument bubbled and fizzed, as though an Alka-Seltzer had been dropped into a glass of water. A more apt metaphor might be that when pure water is poured into a glass with sediment, the fresh flow brings the impurities to the surface, where they're expelled. Something like that happened to me during that drive—a kind of "chemicalization," as I later read. And the migraine dissolved as I allowed this new awareness to percolate through my thoughts.

I graduated from college, moved to New York City a few weeks later, and began looking for ways to find out more about the religion founded by the writer of that book, Mary Baker Eddy. That summer became a cauldron—a time not only of change as I transitioned from student life to full-time career, but a time of taking a stand for my faith before I really knew what it was.

My mother, who'd taken a summer sublet for the family, was apparently terrified that I was being influenced by a cult and seemed to feel I'd be carried off by gypsies if she didn't intervene. Every day she picked a new battle. And on Sunday mornings, when I wanted to attend church services for the first time in my life, she threw tantrums. I began leaving for church an hour early to give her time for these tirades before I headed out the door.

There were no doctrinal points on which I stood, for I didn't know what those points might be for this religion I'd so recently encountered. Nor did I feel there was anything inherently wrong in how my parents thought; indeed I still embrace the same core values they taught me. A visitor had badgered my mother years earlier, asking what religion she and her family practiced. Elegant and polite to a fault, my mother had deftly changed the subject several times. Again, the visitor demanded an answer, and I remember thinking, *No one talks to Mommy like that. This lady's gonna get in trouble.* Sure enough, my mother turned to face her inquisitor and said with authority, "We practice Love in this house." My child heart said, *Go Mommy!* and I stood there beaming.

So this contention that arose between Mom and me during my twenties was a surprise. Tiresome, discouraging, and disappointing though it was, it did nothing to interfere with my forward momentum. I was like a weary traveler who'd asked directions many times and been sent off course. Now I had an abiding sense that I'd found the right road. And that abiding sense was my next experience of faith.

In the decades since, I've come to see faith as the journey from head to heart. For me, it began with logic. I could glimpse a part of Truth and thus deduced that the whole must be true, even if I couldn't see it. Or as Eddy wrote, "We admit the whole because a part is proved, and that part illustrates and proves the entire Principle."[2] In other words, we can grasp that $2 + 2 = 4$. We may not exactly be able to visualize that two million plus two million equals four million, but logic convinces us absolutely that this is true, and we trust this information as factual, foundational—as a rock-solid truth we can return to when we get lost in the abstractions. This part of faith really is like mathematics, and as we work out the problem of Being on our own series of blackboards, the clarity of numbers and our capacity to demonstrate them are as reassuring as geometric proofs.

Then there's another part of faith that sometimes seems as obscure and quixotic as magic. Yet the glimpses that come to us as *feelings* rather than as snippets of logic can be demonstrated just as tangibly. Each of us longs for the experience of manifesting our heart's desire. My own longing is for a sense of integrating my inner life with my outer life—to close the gap between the harmony I envision and the struggle I sometimes experience, and between the huge Love I feel for others and my ability to communicate and share this feeling.

This universal longing has been addressed by sages across time and cultures. "Be really whole, and all things will come to you," wrote Lao Tzu in the sixth century BCE. And in Matthew 6:33, written in the first century CE, we read, "Seek ye first the Kingdom of God . . . and all these things shall be added unto you." These wise ones seem to say we *can* have abundance in whatever way we wish, but that we can't acquire "these things" just by wanting them. They have to come when we're not looking for them, but when we're looking for something more substantial.

So what is substance? Intriguingly, this leads back to faith, as in "Faith is the substance of things hoped for, the evidence of things not seen." (Hebrews 11:1) When this passage first struck me, I was most aware that what was "not seen" in my life was a lasting romantic relationship. After struggling through serial monogamy, divorce, a miscarriage, and a broken engagement, I was ready to concede that the love I desired to give and receive would never happen in this lifetime. To confirm my suspicions, and to begin looking for a different way to structure my life, I called upon a Christian Science teacher and practitioner who asked me a question: "Do you believe that Love comes and goes?"

She used Love with a capital *L*, referring to Eddy's teaching that this is one of the synonyms for God. My first answer was glib. Of *course* I didn't believe that Love—God, the center of the Universe— came and went. He/She/It was the only constant! Yet, as I examined my heart, I realized this was exactly what I'd been believing: that I lived in a universe where Love and Truth, where Principle and Soul would sometimes make a dramatic appearance and then just as inexplicably disappear. I retraced my steps, went back to the metaphysical math, and a fog began to lift.

Of what did the fog consist? Of fears and doubts—some my own, some my parents', some our culture's. Behind that fog lay a more profound truth: that I was inextricably a part of the universe itself, with a mission and purpose only I could fulfill. I ceased looking for an external solution to companionship, and began experiencing my own completeness. The astonishing result was that "all these things" were indeed added to my experience. Within the year, I met and married a wonderful man with whom I continue to experience a loving and solid partnership.

As a young child, I had tiptoed on ice skates along a frozen stream in the Connecticut woods. Though I was alone, I felt accompanied by a Presence—a guiding force that I could trust absolutely—so that as I placed each foot, using the jagged front edge of my skates on the ice ahead, I knew I wouldn't break through to the frigid water flowing beneath the hard surface. I knew I'd find my way through the woods safely. I fervently believe that those of us who earnestly seek this sense of trust will find it in our own language, our own way, our own time.

Faith has continued to be a journey, though I've known it by other names: trust, diligence, conviction, wonderment, awe. Each experience—each demonstration of the truth I've glimpsed—teaches me to trust this inner sense not less, but more. Thus, faith, for me, becomes a stepping stone to understanding on a path that leads out of the finite and into the infinite.

Robotic Love

Dianne Rinehart

I can sadly see where this is going as I listen to the news report about an *outed* robot.

The male *finders* have asked the female *telemarketer* to say, "I am not a robot." Instead, she giggles girlishly, hesitates, and says, "I am a real person."

Again she is challenged. "Just say, 'I am not a robot.'"

Long pause. Nervous laughter. "I am a real person."

The men outing her on the newscast sound, well, like they're *flirting* with her.

In the end, she turns out to be a computer program made up of prerecorded comments selected by a real person. Hence, no access to the phrase, "I am not a robot."

Still, the flirting was real enough. The men were definitely intrigued.

As if it weren't tough enough out there in Relationship Land, now we've got robots to contend with. It wasn't so bad in 1982's *Blade Runner* when Harrison Ford flew off into the sunset with his replicant, the exquisitely beautiful Sean Young, because it just seemed so farfetched.

But now, in real life, we have the flirty *telesales* robots.

And of course, the not-yet-real but equally disturbing star of the movie *Her*. She's an operating system voiced by Scarlett Johansson. To give you a taste of what women will be up against from male robotics designers: her user falls in love with her. When they have hot, virtual phone sex, she even conveniently climaxes for him, and he hasn't had to do a ding-dang thing but take care of himself.

The theme throughout this movie (if it's not in-your-face clear from that scene) is that a computer won't make the demands on a man made by a real woman.

And sure enough, I think back a few years to *The Stepford Wives* (check out the 1975 version if you really want the minus-forty chill effect), and I see a theme that isn't that farfetched.

Until now, I've had faith—faith that men would still want real women—but not the kind of faith that God is going to hand deliver me a partner in crime. Yet here I am, living proof that while there are no simple answers to tough questions when you don't believe in God, there is faith.

Buckets of faith filled to the brim, sloshing out, making a mess of things, soaking everything and everyone in sight. *Look out guys, she's ovulating!*

Really, it might be easier to have had less faith. But I've had to work with the hand that was dealt me. Until recently, I've been a born optimist—a sunny personality in the face of constant challenges. My sister once asked me how I could possibly be so naïve about people after all the hits I've taken. Blind luck? Stupidity?

I'd say faith.

Sadly, this combination of not believing in God while being totally submerged in faith and optimism is a deadly combination when it comes to dating. Especially now that robots are on the scene.

Not that it was easy prerobots. A test drive down memory lane reminds me just how tough dating can be, and this when I'm simply demanding a little information!

He's looking out the window, not at me, when he says, "I can't do this." Tonally, it sounds matter-of-fact, though the message is a thunderclap.

My mouth engages before my brain, and I say with disbelief (and okay, maybe a bit challengingly, because I'm a fighter), "What! You can't answer my question? Where are we going with this?" I repeat.

"I can't do *this*," he emphasizes, louder now, and he is across the room, his boots tied, his jacket on, before I can take in he is leaving. Midconversation. Midsentence.

Holy shit!

I jump up to give him a hug good-bye, but he's already turning his back to me and opening the door. A sound, a yelp, emerges from my belly, my heart, my head.

Last night we made love—slow, sweet, deep.

Today he's walking out without even a good-bye gesture?

He hears my *crie de coeur*, catches my backward movement. He's literally knocked me off-balance with the shock of this sudden change that strikes me, as a friend once described, like a puck attack, a shot to the heart.

He sees this, and something . . . not a lot . . . clicks, as if he's remembering his manners . . . maybe—definitely not responding to his heart. He gives me a hug, but it is so flaccid, so without feeling, so obligatory, it makes me feel worse.

And when he puts his lips to my cheek, it's not really a kiss as much as a movement he might make as a courtesy to an old aunt. It's sexless, emotionless, heartless.

I feel I've already been dusted off and I pull back from him, an indignant squeak escaping my lips. Then I'm mute. If this is the end, where is the tenderness of acknowledgement, even in parting, that we are two human beings who apparently were attracted, dated, laughed, leaped for the bed in anticipation?

This time I do not lean out of my doorway to watch him as he walks down the hall to the elevator, taking pleasure as he invariably turns to flash his Tom Cruise–style smile. I lock the door behind him.

What else was fake?

A week later, I'm on the phone with my younger brother, trying to explain this scene. "Mikey, he was like Flash Gordon. One minute he's contemplating my question, the next nanosecond he's dressed and out the door. He could have won an Olympic competition for flash dressing," I say, trying to pull some humor out of the situation, to unlock the knot in my stomach and regain some dignity, to dampen the humiliation that I feel, because at this stage of life, and after all I've learned, I so utterly and completely misread this man.

Or did I? I hang on to a hope and a prayer that I'm mistaken.

Then it occurs to me that since I didn't watch him, I don't know whether he actually took the elevator. "Maybe he was so panicked, he fled down all twenty-two flights of stairs," I joke.

Mikey finds this very amusing. He begins to make Road Runner beeping sounds, and I, too, am amused by the image of this man flying down the stairs, two at a time, feet whirling, beeping at each landing.

"I bet he slid down the banister," I say, upping the ante. "The doorman probably saw smoke coming off the soles of his shoes as he fled through the lobby."

Though there is momentary relief in joking about the pain that, one week later, is still gnawing at my gut like a rat on cheese, my brother has no answers for me on why a man *I know*—and have known for a long time—might think I'd want to get sexually but not emotionally involved with him.

I am not a robot.

Where the hell does that no-demand concept come from? I don't even understand it when men pick up women in bars. But that's a long way from this relationship of two people who know each other well and reconnect after decades of mutual friends and history.

My friend Alan reminds me that he has repeatedly warned me not to get too emotionally involved with men. "They're all pigs," he says. This is our joke, because he is a man who has been hurt by men.

And this, too, is the crux of all the grieving, wailing, and whining I hear when women gather over dinner to talk, invariably—no matter what else of importance is going on in our lives—about men.

We joke that if we've been dating for six months (that's too much like a serious relationship!), the guy will freak and flee.

We caution each other not to push the envelope (certainly not to ask for information and make demands!) and try to go with the flow.

"Can't you just enjoy it for what it is?" asks my girlfriend (who's been married to the same guy for twenty years and can't remember how she felt dating him before they were married) one night in the lead-up to The Conversation.

"Not if he just wants sex and isn't interested in me."

She argues that this is clearly not the case.

But why live in doubt? Why avoid being clear about what you're both looking for?

Why waste a moment with someone who has already decided he has no intention of doing anything but robotically date you once a week, as long as you don't make any demands? Why make yourself sick with anxiety that the needle on the gauge of your relationship has not moved up one iota since you became intimate; that you don't know what he does or who he's with when he's not with you; that he doesn't call or email except to set up the next date, at which point he shows up as if the previous coupling was yesterday and you can pick up where you left off?

What about the endless internal arguments that are draining every ounce of your creativity and peace of mind? (*Well, he's a great guy. We have fun, he's tender in bed. It must be that he's taking it slowly . . . zzzzz . . .*)

That doesn't work.

You know in your heart there's something wrong, but you are caught between losing him when you speak your mind or ask a question (guy-think for making a demand) and not having him—*really* having him—anyway, because you don't.

So you take a chance. We're adults. Women have rights in a relationship. It's a democracy, yes?

Anyway, best to know whether I'm imagining that he's putting up barriers to a relationship or if he really is.

There's that slim possibility—that pot at the end of a rainbow—that he's actually going to say, "I'm sorry, you're right. I was scared. Let's talk and figure out how we can both get comfortable enough to move forward cautiously, and gently, and joyfully."

Sounds less real than the possibility that a man could fall for his robot, right?

How fucked up is that?

Who knew that his fear or lack of attraction—I still don't know which it was—was on such a grand scale that the breaking down of barriers would mean an immediate breakdown in communication.

Finito. Caput. Ne robota—over one question?

My girlfriend Suz tries to tell me it's about him, not me. He's messed up. And that's true: He told me before leaping across my living room to the door that he's not ready for a relationship—that it's too soon since his marriage breakup *two years ago*. That he's afraid. Funny, he didn't mention that before seducing me. Or perhaps he wasn't afraid of being intimate, just of talking about it?

Suz says it doesn't matter which it is because he doesn't deserve to have an opinion. "He didn't give you a big enough role," she tells me. "Not even a speaking part!"

This, along with her description of him "jackrabbiting," makes me roar with laughter.

She's right. I begin to joke that he's held this as his ace in the hole. "Open your mouth and I walk!" was the unspoken threat. Unspoken, like so much else, but I knew it was there.

And I begin to think there's a TV series here: *Open Your Mouth and I Walk!* Week after week of women trying to figure men out and meekly trying not to be, God help us, demanding, even as we negotiate billion-dollar deals in a boardroom, head up utility companies, are CFOs of publishing houses, or put our lives on the line covering war zones for poorly paying newspapers.

My nephew, whom I confide in over dinner, thinks this idea has potential but says that for one week, after about eleven episodes, we would have to do it the opposite way around, to show a woman doing it to a man.

Ah, sweet revenge.

Except that's not what we want.

We just want a little tenderness.

• ——— •

Maybe this robot thing can be a two-way street.

Can a robot deliver tenderness? Would a robot flee a conversation? Can a robot make love with passion or would it be, umm, robotic?

Would a robot be the kind of guy you can depend on? Or would he all of a sudden want to date a newer model?

But he'd clean up around the house, right? Maybe not. By the time things really got going, the woman would probably be offering to pick up his socks to make sure she didn't get ditched and then have to go back to dating human men who can't answer questions.

I can't see it. No robot holds an attraction for me.

But I'm getting nervous, because I've run this past some nice—I mean *really* nice—guys I know and they kind of smile when I ask them if they could date a robot.

So I'll take a while, dust myself off, accept his apology that comes a month or so too late by email, and drink that cocktail of faith—in men, in myself . . . and in fantasy.

In the end, men would want a real woman, right?

Right?

The Balance

Amanda Enayati

"Welcome to the Suspicious Persons' Booth," says a youngish Arab woman with a halo of black frizz she has attempted to tuck into a hijab the color of dried mud. She is splayed across one of a handful of plastic chairs closest to the entrance.

At first I'm not sure whether she is speaking to me or someone else. I have just stepped into a small room, off in the far corner of the Israeli Customs Hall, enclosed by frosted-glass walls. My American husband has followed me inside, though I was the only one sent here. A moment before, the room's handful of occupants had been staring with varying levels of interest at a football game unfolding on a large wall-mounted television screen. Now they are all staring at the two of us.

My neck and jaw begin aching during the walk over. I'm feeling
a vague guilt without any clue as to why. As if I am my ten-year-old
self once again, in a near-stranger's house, ever dreading that I may
break something or ruin something or use too much of something.

The Arab woman's odd greeting feels like a familiar embrace,
flooding me with a most irrational sense of relief. It stays with me
through the long stretch during which I am vetted by the dour Israeli
customs agent—a squat, burly young man who ignores my husband
and volleys a dozen rapid questions at me, the Iranian-born American
citizen. I worry that my answers sound too well rehearsed.

When the agent is finally satisfied that I do not intend to blow up
any person or thing in his country, he disappears into a back room.

"Where you from?" asks the frizzy woman. Her tone is friendly
and yet her query makes my jaw tense all over again.

As many times as I have been asked where I'm from over the
past several decades, it still stuns me into a bewildered silence as I
try to discern what it is the questioner really wants to know: Where
was I born? Where do I live now? Where do I hold citizenship?

It's all rather complicated, and so it takes me too long to
answer—long enough that the pause is interpreted as an impolite
refusal to respond. I see that the woman's eyes have hardened into a
squint. Or perhaps it's a sneer.

I am a refugee.

I speak the words in my head but can't manage them out loud.
And perhaps it's better that way, because I recognize immediately
that it's a nonsensical answer to the question she asked since *refugee*
is not a place you can be from. But more than any single nation that
I have been chased out of or passed through or lived in for a while,
the word *refugee* begins to describe my provenance.

Because even now, thirty-plus years after the Islamic Republic
of Iran was sealed and delivered by the Iranian Revolution, ejecting
me from my homeland because my family and I belong to a reli-

gious minority the ruling clerics saw (and see) as heretics, I continue to identify myself as a person untethered, homeless in some essential, difficult-to-describe way.

Where am I from?

I am from nowhere. And everywhere.

I have been regarding the Arab woman for so long without uttering a sound that she has decided I am unbalanced. She has gone back to watching football but with her right hand now resting on the side of her head facing me, fingers on her temple, shielding her eyes and doing their best to form a wall between the two of us.

It's all rather awkward. I feel myself flush and a band of perspiration forms on my upper lip. I wipe at the sweat moustache with my sleeve and close my eyes for a minute.

•———•

In my very last memory of Iran, I am also in an airport, except this one is in Tehran, not Tel Aviv.

I'm trotting, holding Baba's hand. He's not walking particularly fast, but he's six foot two—unusually tall for an Iranian—and his legs are twice the length of mine. For each stride he takes, I must take two or three.

There are people everywhere, men and women in a frenzy, agitated like overheated molecules. Maman lags behind, as always. I keep looking back because I'm afraid of losing her in the crowds.

I'm flying out. I'm flying out alone.

"When am I going to see you?"

I'm desperate not to cry.

"Soon. We will come soon."

Their smiles are too big, too eager—like the frozen puppet grins that have always terrified me.

The nights have been grim for weeks now. As dusk settles, a hush blankets the neighborhoods. And then, as it grows dark, a low hum begins to rise like a lost spirit wandering the earth, howling to make itself known. The hum becomes louder and falls into a rhythm: "*Marg bar Shah. Marg bar Shah.*"

Death to the Shah.

And sometimes: "*Allah'u'Akbar. Allah'u'Akbar.*"

God is Great.

They're up on the rooftops, chanting. For hours. Every night now. I wonder if they're on our rooftop as well. I wonder how they get up there. The chanting surrounds us. Permeates our thoughts, our movements, the air we breathe, the space we occupy. It begins to suffocate. We move slowly, quietly, through the chants. We try to go to bed early to escape them but they linger, even in our dreams.

Maman and Baba exchange many looks but no words when I am present. They think I don't see.

In class one day my teacher asks the children who are not Muslim to raise their hands. A half-dozen hands go up, mine among them.

"Tell me which religion you belong to," she demands.

My mind reels. *Allah'u'Akbar!* My body floods with fear. *Marg bar Shah!*

God is great! I don't want to die!

When it's my turn to speak, I hesitate for one instant only. "Jewish," I say.

Is that better than Baha'i? Might that get you killed also? I don't know.

Another child nearby whispers a protest. She knows I'm lying. I'm sure the teacher knows too.

A few weeks later, on the way home, my school bus is intercepted by demonstrators—hundreds of men, with a few pockets of women here and there.

The bus begins to rock like a tugboat caught in an ocean of rage. The bus driver cracks his window and alternates between yelling profanities and quoting passages from the Quran.

Looking back, what strikes me most is the children's silence—frozen, all of us, like small, wide-eyed statues sitting before an angry Medusa.

At some point, the bus door opens. Two adults I don't recognize hurry us out the door and over to a hotel just across the square. The crowd parts all around us—above, below—like a tunnel in a wave that may or may not collapse at any moment. We march in an orderly line of twos, as if we're on an excursion to the museum, pausing only for an instant at the loud crash. Our bus has been turned over and set on fire. The crowd offers up a cheer, not unlike when someone scores a goal at a big football match.

We are ushered into a room at the hotel. They serve us orange soda in paper cups. I look around but do not see our bus driver.

It's the last time I go to school. My school for Iran's gifted children, who were to grow up to serve Iran. Or serve the Shah—I forget which.

•———•

My parents and I arrive at the gate at Tehran airport. I'm handed over to a blond flight attendant in a short blue dress and a matching blue hat that looks like a small, capsized boat.

I have searched for years now, but I have no picture of the next moments. I assume there are hugs and kisses good-bye. I assume there are tears. I assume there are promises of quick reunions.

This is a problem for me. I can't seem to recall this most fateful juncture in my history. Somehow I never recognized it for what it was: Monumental. Irrevocable. My mind failed to capture it adequately, and so it is lost.

Here's what I know for sure: I am a child. I am a Baha'i. It is 1978.

That's how long ago I left.

And I never returned.

•———•

A half-dozen heads snap up as the second Israeli customs agent returns to the Suspicious Persons' Booth bearing papers. The room holds its collective breath, only to exhale a defeated sigh as the agent strides toward me and places my passport back into my hand.

"You may go now," says the agent, nary a smile nor an apology for the long wait.

My husband and I hurry out of Customs. We exit through a pair of automatic glass doors and out into the world beyond.

It is my first time back in the Middle East since the revolution. I am here for a pilgrimage to the Baha'i holy shrines on Mount Carmel in Haifa, my Catholic husband in tow. We left our small children back in the States with my mother because I have business here. Some unanswered questions.

A Russian friend we made on the flight is waiting for us just outside the doors.

"Welcome to Israel," he says. "The *sharaf* is blowing." The sharav (with the *v* pronounced like an *f*) is the hot, dry desert wind that has turned the late afternoon air into a comfortable seventy-five degrees. *Sharav* means something in Farsi, but I cannot recall what.

I smell the air. I'm so close to my homeland that I am almost breathing its oxygen.

By the time we arrive in Haifa, it is dark. And as we begin our ascent up Mount Carmel, I remember that *sharav* means honor.

•———•

I am virtually orphaned by the Islamic Revolution.

For the next five years, I wander, mostly without my parents, around European countries—Holland, Scotland, Germany, England, France—skipping between relatives' houses and a boarding school. I don't stay anyplace more than a year. I've been asked dozens of times whether this was traumatic. At the time it seems more fun than anything else. The emotional impact does not surface for decades.

By the time both my parents finally escape the Mullahs and we all join my older brother in Southern California in the mid-1980s, our family chemistry has changed fundamentally, profoundly. Even as a child in Iran I had been a little different, but now I emerge as a full-blown black sheep, both at home and outside. I speak my mind freely. I always wear black. I sport a Flock of Seagulls hairdo and frosted pink lipstick. I sometimes stay out past 8:00 PM.

But at some point, I lose both my compass and my will. Though I can't manage to harness any image of myself as a lawyer, I escape L.A. to attend law school on the East Coast. I console myself by vowing to practice civil- or human-rights law, but the only people recruiting on campus are big law firms. I am at the top of my class and have my share of high-salary, big-firm offers. Law school has been a blast. Being a lawyer is not.

I am a capable lawyer but an unhappy, most reluctant one. Years pass, my mind numbing with the Novocain of law practice. It's a painful, long-drawn-out quicksand. Inch by inch, I am disappearing.

In 1999 I meet a man—a tall, earnest Mexican American from Texas who's in Washington, DC, working for the Clinton administration. One disastrous date and two makeup dates later, I am in love. He's not Iranian, but my parents adore him—and not just because I've waited so long that they will take anything with a pulse. Two years later, we marry.

We move to New York City in 2000. We live in the West Village on the corner of Sixth and Bleecker. I don't have a job or a clue what to do. In early 2001 I start having night terrors, all having to do with war and disaster in New York. My bewildered husband wakes me up from most of them around 4:00 AM. He thinks it may be some sort of a belated post-traumatic-stress reaction to the revolution.

I freefall into a deep funk. By summer 2001, my panic hits a
fever pitch. On September 10, 2001, I am at a therapist's office,
trying with great difficulty to explain my hysteria. I demand meds.
She promises a referral to a psychiatrist who can prescribe them.
I go home that night thinking that everything will be all right. The
following morning, I stand on Sixth Avenue with a throng of my
fellow New Yorkers as my nightmares come true in a multisensory
horror show.

We move uptown to the Upper West Side. I have a daughter and
then a son. There is a brief magical, carefree period with the babies.
My husband receives a job offer, and we leave our beloved New
York City for the Bay Area.

Problem is, the nightmares have returned. This time I know
what's coming, so I begin preparing. I hoard bottled water and canned
goods. The night terrors involve radiation, so I buy radiation pills on
the internet—one box for us and another for my parents. I start fixat-
ing on the months of August and September of 2007. I refuse to move
into San Francisco proper, reasoning that terrorists will target the big
cities but not the burbs.

We settle on a sunny city on the Peninsula. My husband, toddler, baby, and I arrive in July. In August, disaster strikes, just as I
predicted. Not in the form of a terrorist attack, though.

I am diagnosed with late-stage breast cancer. In my thirties. No
family history. No risk factors. No explanations. *Nothing*. I had been
right about the radiation, but in the end the only person who is irradi-
ated is me.

• ———— •

And now I give you a commandment, which shall
be for a covenant between you and me—that ye
have faith; that your faith be steadfast as a rock that

no storms can move, that nothing can disturb, and
that it endure through all things even to the end;
even should ye hear that your Lord has been crucified, be not shaken in your faith; for I am with
you always, whether living or dead, I am with you
to the end. As ye have faith so shall your powers
and blessings be. This is the balance—this is the
balance—this is the balance.[1]

My business here in the Middle East, in Israel, in Haifa relates
to this particular passage from the Baha'i writings.

I have pored over these lines for two and a half years now, since
I was diagnosed with cancer, reading and rereading them.

I am in desperate need of answers for questions I have about
faith.

Because I have known with an absolute certainly for a few years
now that I no longer have any.

• ———— •

The mastectomy of my right breast takes place in September
2007. The tumor is enormous—9.5 centimeters—and so they also
remove some muscle from my right chest to ensure they have clean
margins around the mass.

I don't recall much about the day of the operation. My father,
husband, and I drive down to Stanford Hospital at dawn. My mother
remains home with the children.

The ride is somber. I try to lighten the mood, and so does my
father. He's a tall, lanky, happy-go-lucky kind of guy. Which is why
it is so heartbreaking that the last thing I remember is sitting in a
wheelchair, being wheeled backward, a door closing on my dad, and
his smile melting into tears in one fluid movement.

I remember nothing else.

Until I wake up.

I am at the bottom of a well, with people peeking down at me. And then they fade away.

When I wake again, my mother is sitting to my left. I cannot move. But even worse, I can't *breathe*.

I had never noticed how much effort it takes to raise your chest, expand your lungs. Inhale. Then exhale.

I struggle with these, so I take short, shallow breaths that require minimal physical exertion, but which also means that I never feel completely satisfied with the amount of air I am taking in. I am starving for air. I am drowning.

Every part of my body hurts.

I can't move.

I cannot move.

I am in this world but only by a thread, as if I am perfectly capable of slipping away.

So I do the only thing I can. I grab my mother's hand and hold on for my life, so that I won't drift off.

•———•

We are due at the Pilgrim House by noon the morning after we arrive in Israel. Baha'i pilgrims trickle in from every corner of the planet— an odd, mismatched community—sitting elbow to elbow, mother next to son next to father next to daughter.

A few days later, on a day trip to Jerusalem, I will recall this scene during a visit to the Garden of Gethsemane at the foot of the Mount of Olives. The site is where Jesus Christ spends his last hours as a free man. It is in this garden that Jesus, betrayed by his disciple Judas, is captured by Roman soldiers and sent on the path that leads to his crucifixion.

The Romans want to arrest him when he's not surrounded by too many people. Jesus knows what's coming to pass, so he sits atop what is known as the Rock of Agony, praying, asking why—why must he be tested in this way?

There is a grove of ancient olive trees at the Garden of Gethsemane. The first time you see these thousand-year-old trees, it looks as if there are many of them crowded into tight plots. But when you step forward to take a closer look, you see that what appear to be clusters of four or five separate gnarled tree trunks, each reaching toward the sky in a different direction, are really branches of the same tree.

You can stand there and trace each branch to the body of the one tree—solid, steadfast, rooted deep into the earth.

And there we all sit, pilgrims in the Pilgrim House, in silence for the eternity of a moment, breathing in unison.

Like branches of one tree.

One body, divided only by perception.

Under God.

Indivisible.

This unity—this essential oneness—is the essence of my faith and the faith of my forefathers (four generations on my father's side and four generations on my mother's). My faith is innate and steeped in my soul—so much so that as a child my mother often refers to me as "the *Mullah*."

The Baha'i faith is founded in Shiraz, Iran, in 1844 when a man named Siyyid Ali-Muhammad foretells the coming of a great prophet who will herald a new age. He is a sort of John the Baptist, if you will. He eventually becomes known as the Báb, which means *the Gate*. He is executed six years later in the city of Tabriz. In 1863 one of the Báb's followers, Baha'u'llah (Arabic for "Glory of God"), declares himself to be the messenger promised by the Báb. Baha'u'llah's message: humankind is one and all religions teach the same truth. He is exiled for years and eventually dies as a prisoner in what was then Palestine.

Our group of pilgrims is scheduled to visit the garden of Bahji, the site of the Shrine of Baha'u'llah. The bus deposits us at the end of a long gravel road. Our feet crunch on the approach to the ornate double doors, protected by a black and gold awning. We are requested to take off our shoes and leave them outside. There is a basket of prayer books, but I have brought my own.

We walk through, enveloped by silence and the scent of roses. Several of the other pilgrims are quickly overcome by emotion. I hold myself rigid, stony, committed to absolute authenticity, unmoved—and unmovable—by sentiment. I settle cross-legged into a small prayer space to the left of the shrine. And I wait.

•————•

Unlike many families I know, mine doesn't have a tradition of storytelling.

Which is why it's so curious that at some point during that dark year of cancer, when my mother comes to live with us, she tells me a story. She tells it unsolicited, out of the blue one day.

She says she was always a serious, studious girl. She had very good grades. She dreamed big dreams and didn't pay attention to anyone, especially not boys.

"There were lots of girls out in the streets," she says, "but I was a good girl."

In the middle of her final year of school, she is trying to figure out what to do with her life. Her father has already sent her two younger brothers overseas to study.

My mother thinks she would make a good doctor, but no one seems particularly interested in her or her career plans. So she takes it upon herself to look around to see whether there are any possibilities.

She finds a two-year fellowship funded by the British government at a local hospital. The program will culminate in medical training in obstetrics in England.

My mother signs herself up, studies for weeks, takes the entrance examination, and is eventually offered a spot.

Acceptance in hand, she goes to ask her father for permission to attend.

"Absolutely not," he says, "no daughter of mine is going to fall under the paws of the doctors at a hospital."

And that is that.

"I would have been a good doctor," is all she says in conclusion.

I am enraged, as if it had all happened the day before yesterday and not a half century ago.

"Don't be angry," she says. "He was a great father and a kind man."

I think about my mother and her life. I think about dashed hopes and unrealized dreams, and how they stagnate. And become diseased and hardened with time, leeching into your bloodstream, your soul, invading your cells with despair and negativity until you don't remember a time when you didn't feel that way. Until you can no longer tell the difference between the bitterness and the real you.

And you forget about *before*, when you were a fresh spirit, standing on the precipice of a joyful, magical adventure; ready to step off, giddy, anticipating the flight; bracing for the adversities that would surely lie ahead. But mostly wondering how it will feel to see the world from far above, the wind in your face, rushing through your hair. Marveling at the possibilities.

And then flying.

Flying.

•————•

"As ye have faith so shall your powers and blessings be. This is the balance," reads the Baha'i passage I held close for years.

But I am no longer interested in the balance between faith and blessings. I wish to understand the balance between faith and suffering. I sit hunched over in the Shrine of Baha'u'llah, reciting prayer after prayer, each supplication stained with tears and accusation, betrayal and rage: I believed. I believed. Why did you forsake me?

•————•

Gaining a devout following in a short period of time, the Báb is imprisoned and sentenced to death for being a heretic, a traitor to Islam.

On the date of his execution, he is in his cell with his amanuensis when the guards come to take them to the firing squad. The Báb declares that he is not ready to go, as he is not yet finished with the tablet he is revealing. He is taken forcibly from the prison cell and placed before the executioners on a public square. A large crowd of thousands throngs rooftops and windows of the public square, all gathered to watch him die.

The firing squad, a regimen of 750 Armenian Christian troops, takes its place, aims, and fires. The smoke from the rifles kicks up a massive cloud of dust, shrouding the square in darkness. When the dust clears, the Báb is gone, as is his aide. The authorities begin a frenzied search. They find him back at his cell, completing his final instructions to his secretary. He looks up calmly and announces: I am ready.

They take him and his young aide, shackled this time, before the firing squad. The problem is that the Christian regimen, recognizing what they just saw and fearing the wrath of God, refuse to fire on him again. And so the authorities have to go through the trouble of finding yet a second squadron to fire. Not an easy task during a time of no telephone, email, or fax. Eventually a Muslim squadron is procured and the task is done. This time, the Báb and his assistant are killed. It is noted after the execution that though their bodies are riddled with bullets, not one bullet has as much as grazed either of their faces.

Here's the thing about miracles: they only really belong to the people who are there to witness them—who perceive them with their own senses. Everyone else either accepts it on faith or as a mighty good story.

•————•

Hours later I leave the Shrine of Baha'u'llah, prayer book in hand, wounded, devastated, finally broken wide open.

I have my answer.

It comes to me in the form of a single verse from a mystic. I have known this verse even as a child, but it has been buried many layers beneath self-pity and oblivion, denial and withdrawal.

"The wound," wrote Rumi, "is where the light enters you."

•————•

I want to tell you about a miracle. You are free to accept it as true or as a good story.

It is the tale of a young girl, a child of faith, turned out from her home for no good reason, separated from her kin, tormented for decades by what life delivered at her doorstep—a virtual encyclopedia of tragedy: revolution, disease, isolation, dysfunction, terrorism, failure, and withdrawal. You also ought to know that if you were to meet this girl, you might think that a sunnier person never lived.

Eventually she grew numb—this girl—extinguished and faithless, consumed again and again by the fires that threatened to destroy her.

Until she realized that they didn't.

They did not and had not destroyed her.

The devilry seared, yes, but the burn, the agony, the pain had only made her stronger, more powerful.

She looked inward and saw that beneath those wounds she burned bright, like a dozen suns.

She burned with wrath, with fury. She burned with justice and compassion and love. And she burned, once again, with faith.

With nothing else to lose, she dared, finally, to approach the precipice she had feared the most, so that perhaps she might embark upon the most magical adventure of her life. When she stepped off the rock, she did so giddily, anticipating the flight and bracing for the adversities that would surely lie ahead, but mostly wondering how it would feel to see the world from far above, the wind in her face, rushing through her hair. Marveling at the possibilities.

Then she took flight.

She realized, as she flew, that her powers and blessings had grown in proportion to her faith. That her faith had solidified through the suffering. And that this had been the balance all along.

In Closing

Recently I was visiting a new friend in her home. When we sat down for dinner, I sensed a sudden quiet and realized she was offering a silent prayer. When she was finished, I asked, "If I weren't here, would you pray in silence?" She told me no, that she prayed aloud, but was respecting my beliefs. (She is a devout Mormon; I am a reformed Jew.) When we shared our next meal, I asked her to pray aloud. "Even the part about Jesus is fine," I added, and she smiled. And then she prayed. I won't say it was a defining moment, but I can say that it was a warm experience between two friends. (She replaced the closing "in the name of Jesus Christ" with "in thy holy name.")

There was one meal, however, when she began to pray and I interrupted with, "It's my turn—may I?" She smiled, and then I prayed.

There was no stumbling along, no searching for that perfect word: a simple thank-you was given for all that grows, nurtures, sustains, and the wish that those I love live with health and joy. It was ten seconds at most, yet after that moment, I could barely eat, so caught off guard was I by my emotions. We've shared many meals since, and I will occasionally recite the prayer (more often I give her an imploring look, and she smiles and prays).

I've thought about that first prayer we shared, wondering if my participation had to do with wanting to please my friend or needing to convince her that I was worthy of the friendship. But what I've come to understand is that prayer is a way for me to hold on to the light, my gratitude, my family, the wonderful life I've been so privileged to live, and see it all more clearly, perhaps feel it more honestly.

I began this book as a way to clarify my beliefs—to answer the one question I stumble upon at every turn: *What do I believe?* I may never know the answer, at least not in the didactic sense, but I'm being driven forward, riding the crest of a wave whose momentum continues to carry me, and hold me aloft and somehow safe from the thundering waters below. What do I expect to find along the way? The ability to free myself from self-doubt, from the confusion that bubbles up as I take those risks that alter the direction of my life.

Whatever it is that causes such roiling in the darkness of the late hours, when it seems that I'm the only one awake in a world of the peacefully sleeping, my challenge is to stay the course, to continue to move toward the light of understanding and knowledge, to remain upright and upstanding, learning and absorbing all that I can until my last moment—the moment of my death…and perhaps beyond.

Acknowledgments

This book came to me while I was driving from Los Angeles to my home in San Francisco. As I zipped past lush fields of fruit trees (early in the drought Central Valley) and corrals of unsuspecting cattle awaiting steak-dom, my thoughts were so focused on the subject of faith that the six-hour drive felt like minutes. By the time I arrived home, the book was formed. I immediately contacted my agent, Jill Marsal, whose instincts and honesty I trust and respect. Without Jill, there is no book. She encouraged me to do it, and that was all I needed. Jill, thank you . . . again.

My next call was to my friend, author Anne Perry, with whom I've shared hundreds (and hundreds) of phone calls and emails regarding faith. Without her support and encouragement, I'm quite sure I would have stumbled over a cliff and taken the idea for this book with me.

I offer my heartfelt thanks to Lee Turicchi and Margo Kuzee for allowing me to tell their very personal stories.

And to Anne Connelly, whose editing eye and heart make me a better writer, I thank you yet again.

When editor Emily Han from Beyond Words bought this book, her enthusiasm and encouragement shot through me like an electric impulse. No matter how complex (or idiotic) my questions, Emily has always responded with warmth and expertise. From our first contact to now, that support has never wavered. For this, and for Emily's dedication to the subject of faith, I am so very grateful.

My unending gratitude to the community of generous and gifted writers who opened their hearts, minds, and souls, entrusting to all of us their poignant, thoughtful, joyful, and sometimes humorous thoughts about a difficult and often controversial subject.

With all my heart, I wish Lee Chamberlin and Leon Whiteson were here to share in our joy.

Notes

Introduction

1. Søren Kierkegaard, BrainyQuote.com, accessed August 6, 2014, http://www.brainyquote.com/quotes/quotes/s/sorenkierk152229 .html.

I

1. Frederick William Henry Myers, "A Last Appeal," *Oxford Book of English Mystical Verse* (Oxford, England: The Clarendon Press, 1917), 337.

Grace Happens

1. Mother Meera, *Answers* (New York: Meeramma Publications, 1991), 74.

2. Ibid.
3. Ibid, 79.

An Itinerary of Faith

1. D. G. Rand Shenhav and J. D. Greene, "Divine Intuition: Cognitive Style Influences Belief in God," *Journal of Experimental Psychology: General* 141, no. 3 (August 2012): 423–8. There is vast scientific literature on this topic, notably by Antonio Damasio, Stanislas Dehaene, and colleagues.
2. Massimo Pigliucci, "On Intuition," *Rationally Speaking* (e-column), no. 29, October 29, 2002, http://chem.tufts.edu /science/pigliucci/rationally-speaking/02-10-on_intuition.htm.
3. G. Vogel. Untitled article, *Science*, 275 no. 5304 (1997): 1269.

Poof!

1. Ian McEwan, *Solar* (New York: Anchor, 2011), 198.
2. Philip Larkin, "Aubade," The Poetry Foundation, accessed August 6, 2014, http://www.poetryfoundation.org/poem/178058.
3. Julian Barnes, *Levels of Life* (New York: Knopf, 2013), 81.

Keep the Faith

1. Arthur J. Scanlan and Patrick Cardinal Hayes, *The Little Catholic Prayerbook for Children* (New York: Catholic Publications Press, 1925).

The F-Word

1. Newsweek Staff, "Does Your iPod Play Favorites?" *Newsweek*, January 30, 2005, http://www.newsweek.com/does-your -ipod-play-favorites-116739.
2. Mark Twain, "A Humorist's Confession," *The New York Times*, November 26, 1905.

Nothing

1. Huffington Post, "Surprising Number of Americans Don't Believe in Evolution," January 23, 2014, http://huffingtonpost.com/2013/12/30/evolution-survey_n_4519441.html.
2. Rachel Weiner, "No-Choice: 87% of U.S. Counties Have No Access to Abortion Clinic," *The Huffington Post*, July 3, 2009, http://www.huffingtonpost.com/2009/06/02/no-choice-87-of-us-counti_n_210194.html.

Faith: A Personal Journey

1. Mary Baker Eddy, *Science and Health with Key to the Scriptures*, authorized study edition (Boston, MA: The Christian Science Board of Directors, 2006), 461–5.
2. Ibid, 383.

The Balance

1. 'Abdu'l-Bahá, "I Am With You Always," *Star of the West* 12, no. 16 (1921): 250.

About the Contributors

Barbara Abercrombie has published novels, children's books, and nonfiction. Her personal essays have appeared in national publications and anthologies. Recent books are *Courage & Craft: Writing Your Life Into Story*; *Cherished: 21 Writers on Animals They've Loved & Lost*; *A Year of Writing Dangerously*, a *Poets & Writers Magazine* choice as a top book for writers; and *Kicking In the Wall*. She was named Outstanding Instructor and given the Distinguished Instructor Award at UCLA Extension, where she teaches creative writing. Barbara also conducts private writing retreats and writes a weekly blog. She lives with her husband and their rescue dog in Santa Monica and Lake Arrowhead.

•———•

Tamim Ansary, Afghan American author and lecturer, writes about politics, democracy, history, philosophy, education, sports, movies, and whatever else catches his fancy. His books include *Games Without Rules* (an epic narrative history of Afghanistan); *The Widow's Husband* (a historical novel set during the first Afghan-British War); and *West of Kabul, East of New York* (a literary memoir chosen by San Francisco as its One City One Book selection for 2008). He also wrote *Destiny Disrupted: A History of the World Through Islamic Eyes*, which won a 2010 Northern California Book Award and has been translated into ten languages.

•———•

Lee Chamberlin was an actress of stage, film, and TV, and was an accomplished playwright, theater director, and essayist. She began her acting career on New York's Off-Broadway stages, performing in *Your Own Thing*, a musical version of Shakespeare's *Twelfth Night*, and appearing in such plays as LeRoi Jones's *Slaveship* at the Brooklyn Academy of Music, and as Cordelia in the New York Shakespeare Festival's *King Lear* (opposite James Earl Jones). She also appeared as guest artist at Penn State University in the title role of the Greek tragedy *Medea*. A member of the original cast of PBS's *The Electric Company*, Lee was a Grammy winner and Emmy nominee. In addition, Lee wrote the book, music, and lyrics of the musical *Struttin'*. As an actress, she made guest appearances on many television series, including *NYPD Blue*, and costarred with James Earl Jones in the series *Paris*. Lee played Madame Zenobia in the film *Uptown Saturday Night*, and costarred with Sidney Poitier and Bill Cosby in *Let's Do It Again*. Her decade-long role as Pat Baxter on *All My Children* made her a recognizable figure in the United States and abroad. Lee was the founder and artistic director of the Playwrights' Inn Project, a Paris-based nonprofit that expands access to the play development process to include African American playwrights. Lee Chamberlin passed away in May 2014.

"Faith" Copyright © 2015 by Lee Chamberlin

•———•

David Corbett is the author of five novels: *The Devil's Redhead*, *Done for a Dime* (a *New York Times* Notable Book), *Blood of Paradise* (nominated for numerous awards, including the Edgar Award), *Do They Know I'm Running?*, and his latest, *The Mercy of the Night* (April 2015). David's short fiction and poetry have appeared in numerous journals and anthologies, including *The Best American Mystery Stories* (2009 and 2011), and his nonfiction has appeared in the *New York Times*, *San Francisco Chronicle*, *Narrative*, *Zyzzyva*, the *Writer*, and *Writer's Digest*. In January 2013, Penguin published his textbook on the craft of characterization, *The Art of Character*.

"Love and Insomnia" Copyright © 2015 by David Corbett

•———•

Beverly Donofrio, recently dubbed a master memoirist by the *Daily Beast*, has published three memoirs: the *New York Times* bestseller *Riding in Cars with Boys*, which was made into a popular movie; *Looking for Mary*, a Barnes and Noble Discover Great New Writers pick; and *Astonished*, called "astonishing" by more than one reviewer. Her three children's books are much praised, her NPR documentaries are perennially rebroadcast, and her personal essays have appeared in the *New York Times*; the *Washington Post*; *Los Angeles Times*; *O, The Oprah Magazine*; *Cosmopolitan*; *Mademoiselle*; *Marie Claire*; *More*; *Allure*; *Spirituality and Health* the *Village Voice*; the *Huffington Post*; *Slate*; as well as numerous anthologies. She's currently at work on a play, with music.

"Choosing" Copyright © 2015 by Beverly Donofrio

•————•

Amanda Enayati is an Iranian American author and columnist, writing on the quest for well-being and life balance during difficult times since the launch of her "Seeking Serenity" series on CNN Health in 2011. Her essays about happiness, creativity, technology, and identity have appeared widely online, in print, and on the radio, including *PBS MediaShift*, the *Washington Post*, *Salon*, *Reader's Digest*, and public radio, among others. Her book, *Seeking Serenity*, was published by Penguin's New American Library in January 2015.

"The Balance" Copyright © 2015 by Amanda Enayati

•————•

Amy Ferris is an author, screenwriter, editor, and playwright. Her memoir, *Marrying George Clooney: Confessions from a Midlife Crisis*, was produced as an Off-Broadway play. She has written screenplays for the films *Mr. Wonderful* (Anthony Minghella, director) and *Funny Valentines* (Julie Dash, director), and several TV series. *Funny Valentines* was nominated for several awards, including best screenplay. She has contributed to numerous anthologies, including *Dancing at the Shame Prom: Sharing the Stories That*

Kept Us Small, which she coedited. She lives in Pennsylvania with her husband, Ken, and their two cats, Bella and Lotus.

"Ah.Yes." Copyright © 2015 by Amy Ferris

•——————•

Susana Franck is an Argentine-born, Paris-based writer and editor who, for thirty-five years, was editorial associate of *Cognition, International Journal of Cognitive Science.* She earned a BA cum laude in French from Bryn Mawr College and studied postgrad at Columbia University before moving to France. A former member of the CNRS Laboratoire de Sciences Cognitives et Psycholinguistique, she has also worked with the neuroscience department of the International School for Advanced Study in Trieste, Italy. Susana has coedited (with Jacques Mehler and Stanislas Dehaene) books in cognitive science.

"An Itinerary of Faith" Copyright © 2015 by Susana Franck

•——————•

Benita (Bonnie) Garvin is an award-winning film and television writer and producer. She also teaches screenwriting at the University of Southern California and the Art Center College of Design in Pasadena. She has film credits in the United States and Europe. Her original film, *The Killing Yard,* premiered at the Toronto Film Festival and was nominated for a number of awards. Her television movie about teenage bullying earned a Directors Guild nomination. Her most recent movie, *Run for Your Life,* aired in October 2014 and explores the impact of domestic violence.

"Nothing" Copyright © 2015 by Benita Garvin

•————•

Barbara Graham is an author, essayist, and playwright. Her books include the *New York Times* bestseller *Eye of My Heart: 27 Writers Reveal the Hidden Pleasures and Perils of Being a Grandmother* and *Camp Paradox: A Memoir of Stolen Innocence*, a recently published eBook. Barbara has contributed to numerous essay collections, websites, and magazines, including *Glamour*; *More*; *National Geographic Traveler*; *O, The Oprah Magazine*; *Time*; *Tricycle*; *Utne Reader*; and *Vogue*. Her plays have been produced Off-Broadway and around the country.

"Grace Happens" Copyright © 2015 by Barbara Graham

•————•

Pam Houston is the author of five books of fiction and nonfiction, including *Cowboys Are My Weakness*, *Sight Hound*, and *Contents May Have Shifted*. She teaches at the University of California, Davis, and is cofounder of a community called Writing By Writers. Her essay "Corn Maze" recently won a Pushcart Prize. Her collection of linked short stories, *Cowboys Are My Weakness*, won the Western States Book Award, and *Waltzing the Cat* won the Willa Award for Contemporary Fiction. Her stories have been selected for the 1999 volumes of *The Best American Short Stories*, *The O. Henry Prize Stories*, and *The Best American Short Stories of the Century*. She is a regular contributor to *O, the Oprah Magazine*; the *New York Times*; *Bark*; *More*; and many other periodicals. Her essays have been widely anthologized and are collected in the volume *A Little More About Me*.

"If There Is a God, Why Would S(He) Waste All Her Time Making Hell?" Copyright © 2015 by Pam Houston

•———•

Carrie (Cariad) Kabak is the author of *Cover the Butter*, an Independent Booksellers Pick, and her essays have appeared in *For Keeps, He Said What?*, and *Exit Laughing*. Her second novel, *Deviled Egg*, is in progress. Carrie is a creative technician at Hallmark Cards, Inc., and a designer for Pan Macmillan and other major publishers. Born and raised in the United Kingdom, Carrie now lives in Missouri with her husband, who is a professional cook and the owner of a specialist food company. They share five sons, two labradors, two cats, and two birds.

"Razor-Edged Abyss" Copyright © 2015 by Carrie Kabak

•———•

Aviva Layton is the author of the novel *Nobody's Daughter* and several children's books. Her essays have appeared in *Essays: Patterns and Perspectives*, *The Other Woman*, *The Face in the Mirror*, and *Exit Laughing*. She has taught literature at universities, colleges, and art schools; and has reviewed plays, books, and film for newspapers, journals, and radio arts programs in the United States and Canada. Born in Sydney, Australia, the author lived for many years in Montreal, Toronto, and London. She currently resides in Los Angeles, where she works as a literary editor. Aviva is the mother of Canadian author David Layton.

"Poof!" Copyright © 2015 by Aviva Layton

•———•

Caroline Leavitt is the *New York Times*– and *USA Today*–bestselling author of *Pictures of You* and *Is This Tomorrow*. A book critic for *People*, the *Boston Globe*, and the *San Francisco Chronicle*, she is also the author of eight earlier novels, including *Girls in Trouble*. She teaches novel writing online for Stanford University and the UCLA Extension Writers' Program. Caroline lives in New Jersey with her husband, music writer Jeff Tamarkin, and their teenage son, Max.

"My Counter-Culture Spirituality: How Sudden Death, Tarot Cards, and Mediums Led Me to Quantum Physics—and Belief" Copyright © 2015 by Caroline Leavitt

•———•

Malachy McCourt is a Brooklyn-born, Limerick-reared author and raconteur who has been a longshoreman, radio personality, film and theater actor, playwright, and in 2006, a Green Party gubernatorial candidate in New York. He wrote *A Monk Swimming*, a United States and international bestseller; *Singing My Him Song*; *Bush Lies in State*; *Malachy McCourt's History of Ireland*; *The Claddagh Ring: Ireland's Cherished Symbol of Friendship, Loyalty, and Love*; *Harold Be Thy Name: Lighthearted Daily Reflections for People in Recovery*; and *Danny Boy: The Legend of the Beloved Irish Ballad*. *A Couple of Blaguards*, the play written with brother Frank McCourt, was published in book form by Welcome Rain, New York.

"I'm an Atheist, Thank God!" Copyright © 2015 by Malachy McCourt

•———•

David Misch is the author of *Funny: The Book—Everything You Always Wanted to Know About Comedy*. He's been a comic folk singer, standup comedian, and screenwriter; his credits include *Mork and Mindy*, *Duckman*, *Police Squad!*, *Saturday Night Live*, and *The Muppets Take Manhattan*. He blogs for the *Huffington Post*, and his play *Occupied* is scheduled to be produced in Los Angeles. He has taught comedy at USC, musical satire at UCLA, and he has lectured at Oxford University, Columbia University, the 92nd Street Y, the Midwest Popular Culture Association Conference, the American Film Institute, and the New York, Chicago, Los Angeles, and Boston public libraries.

• ——— •

Jacquelyn Mitchard has written ten novels, including several *New York Times* bestsellers. She won Great Britain's People Are Talking prize and was on the short list for the Orange Broadband Prize for Fiction. Her essays have appeared worldwide, anthologized and incorporated into school curricula. Jacquelyn contributed to an anthology of short stories which honored her mentor, Ray Bradbury, and won the Bram Stoker and Shirley Jackson Awards. Her first novel, *The Deep End of the Ocean*, was the inaugural selection of the Oprah Winfrey Book Club and later adapted for a feature film. Editor in chief of Merit Press, a young adult fiction imprint, she is also a distinguished fellow at the Ragdale Foundation, and a DeWitt Wallace–*Readers Digest* fellow of the MacDowell Colony. A member of the Lac du Flambeau Cree Chippewa tribe, Jacquelyn lives on Cape Cod with her family.

• ——— •

Christine Kehl O'Hagan is the author of *Benediction at the Savoia*, a novel, and the memoir *The Book of Kehls*. Both received starred reviews in *Kirkus Reviews*, the latter a *Kirkus* Best Book of 2005 selection. Her essays have appeared in *Between Friends*, *The Day My Father Died*, *Lives Through Literature*, *The Facts on File Companion to the American Novel*, *Exploring Literature*, *Quest Magazine*, *For Keeps*, *The Face in the Mirror*, *He Said What?*, *Ploughshares*, the *Sun*, *The Story Within: Personal Essays on Genetics and Identity*, and *Exit Laughing*. She received the Jerry Lewis Writing Award and has contributed to the *New York Times*, *Newsday*, and several Long Island publications. Christine lives on Long Island with her family and is working on a second memoir.

• ———— •

Anne Perry is a *New York Times* and international bestselling author, noted for her memorable characters, historical accuracy, and exploration of social and ethical issues. Two of her series—one featuring Thomas Pitt and one featuring William Monk—have been published in dozens of languages. Anne has also published a third successful series based around World War I and the Reavley family. Among her other novels is the stand-alone, epic Byzantium novel, *The Sheen on the Silk*, and two fantasies reflecting her deep spiritual convictions: *Tathea* and *Come Armageddon*. She has also written two novels set in France during the revolution. Anne has published more than eighty novels and has nearly thirty million books in print, with none of her titles ever having been out of print. A recipient of the prestigious Edgar Award, she was selected by the *Times* as one of the twentieth century's 100 Masters of Crime. She lives in Los Angeles and the northeast highlands of Scotland.

•————•

Mara Purl is the author of the award-winning Milford-Haven series of bestselling novels and short stories set on the California coast. *Milford-Haven, U.S.A.* was the first American radio drama licensed and broadcast by the BBC, enjoyed by 4.5 million listeners in the United Kingdom. She also coauthored *Act Right: A Manual for the On-Camera Actor*, an entertainment-industry bestseller. As an actress, Mara was Darla Cook on *Days of Our Lives*, and as a musician, she plays koto and has released five CDs. Mara was a journalist for the *Financial Times of London*, the Associated Press, *Rolling Stone*, and the *Christian Science Monitor*. Named one of twelve Women of the Year by the Los Angeles County Commission for Women, she speaks for women's groups, including the American Heart Association's Go Red for Women, and conducts her special ChariTea events across the United States. She lives in Los Angeles and Colorado Springs, Colorado.

•————•

Dianne Rinehart has worked in Moscow, Ottawa, Toronto, and Vancouver as an editor, reporter, and columnist for some of the largest newspapers and magazines in Canada and the United States. She is currently an editorial writer at the *Toronto Star*, Canada's largest newspaper. Her work has appeared in the anthologies *He Said What?* and *Exit Laughing*. Dianne has also taught feature writing at Ryerson University in Toronto.

•———•

Sylvie Simmons, the subject of the BBC documentary *The Rock Chick*, is a London-born music journalist, singer, songwriter, and ukulele player and an award-winning author of fiction and non-fiction books, including the short story collection *Too Weird For Ziggy* and a biography of Serge Gainsbourg, *A Fistful of Gitanes*. Her latest book is the *New York Times* and international bestseller *I'm Your Man: The Life of Leonard Cohen*, which NPR's *All Things Considered* named Best Biography of the Year. Her debut album of original songs was released in 2014 on Light in the Attic Records.

•———•

Frank Dabba Smith is the rabbi at Harrow and Wembley Progressive Synagogue in London. He served as chairperson of the Brent Multifaith Forum and currently serves as liaison with the Metropolitan Police, and he works alongside Muslims to teach police officers about Judaism and Islam. He is an active member of the International Advisory Committee of Friends of the Earth Middle East and holds MA degrees in Hebrew and Jewish studies, as well as photographic studies. Frank is writing a PhD dissertation at University College London concerning the camera manufacturer Ernst Leitz of Wetzlar and the efforts to help the persecuted in Nazi Germany. At Leo Baeck College in London, he teaches about the Holocaust and its aftermath, as well as a course on death, dying, and bereavement. Publications include *My Secret Camera* and *Elsie's War* (introduction by Henri Cartier-Bresson). Recent solo photographic-exhibition venues include the Leica Gallery (New York City) and SAK Art Museum (Denmark). He lives in London with his wife and their three children.

•————•

Victoria Zackheim (anthology editor) is the author of the novel *The Bone Weaver*, and editor of five anthologies, the most recent being *Exit Laughing: How Humor Takes the Sting Out of Death*. Her screenplay, *Maidstone*, a feature film, is in development, as are her theater plays *The Other Woman* and *Entangled*. Victoria also writes documentary films and teaches creative nonfiction (personal essay) in the UCLA Extension Writers' Program. She is a 2010 San Francisco Library Laureate.